White Gazpa
Sesame Brea
CLT • Brocco
Pot Macaroni and Cheese • French Pasta Salad •
Sweet Corn Muffins • Tortoni • Pineapple Sherbet•
Monkeys in a Blanket • And Much More!

These 250 mouth-watering short-order recipes are
drawn from traditional American specialties, as
well as from popular ethnic cuisines. They answer
the growing demand for wholesome eating from
today's health-and-time-conscious society. Based
on the use of vegetable proteins, eggs, cheese,
and unrefined foods, these recipes are guaranteed
to impress even the most discriminating palate.

THE GOLDBECKS'
Short-Order
COOKBOOK

NIKKI GOLDBECK has a degree in nutrition from Cornell
University and professional experience in recipe
development.

DAVID GOLDBECK is a lawyer, publisher, and educator.

The Goldbecks have been writing and teaching about
food for over 15 years. Their aim has been to show
people that an enjoyable diet can be a healthful one;
their work has earned them the respect and support of
major health and consumer groups. Previous Goldbeck
bestsellers include, in addition to *Nikki & David Goldbeck's
American Wholefoods Cuisine, The Supermarket
Handbook* and *The Goldbecks' Guide to Good Food.*
They also write the "Naturally Fast" column for
Vegetarian Times.

THE GOLDBECKS'
Short-Order
COOKBOOK

Nikki & David Goldbeck

Excerpted from
NIKKI AND DAVID GOLDBECK'S
AMERICAN WHOLEFOODS CUISINE

A SIGNET BOOK

NEW AMERICAN LIBRARY

In memory of Kurt Julius Goldbeck

SIGNET TRADEMARK REG. U.S. PAT. OFF. AND FOREIGN COUNTRIES

REGISTERED TRADEMARK—MARCA REGISTRADA

HECHO EN CHICAGO, U.S.A.

SIGNET, SIGNET CLASSIC, MENTOR, ONYX, PLUME, MERIDIAN and NAL BOOKS are published by NAL PENGUIN INC., 1633 Broadway, New York, New York 10019

First Printing, March, 1988

1   2   3   4   5   6   7   8   9

PRINTED IN THE UNITED STATES OF AMERICA

Contents

Introduction:
Short-Order Cooking

Short-order cooking implies meals made with a minimum of effort, and for this reason, a short-order dish must have only a few ingredients and be simple to assemble. Happily, such convenience translates easily to wholefoods cooking.

For many reasons, traditional short-order cooking does not enjoy a particularly good reputation. Too often the quality of ingredients is marginal and the knowledge of cooking techniques minimal; deep-frying and overcooking are part of the tradition, as are highly processed foods. But, at one time or another, the idea of cooking good luncheonette-diner-drugstore meals appeals to everyone. Most people enjoy, at least occasionally, fulfilling their kitchen fantasies by turning out omelets, grilled and overstuffed sandwiches, or bowls of chili.

This book is devoted to promoting the best of this institution and demonstrating how even straightforward recipes can be served with style.

In addition to bringing out the short-order chef in you, this book is designed to assist the restaurateur. We are beginning to see the emergence of "wholefoods diners" in the United States that provide wholesome, reasonably priced food, like the dishes served up here. Hopefully this is a trend.

> —Nikki and David Goldbeck
> *August 1987*

The Short-Order Kitchen

Your food inventory need not be extensive. "The Short-Order Pantry," which appears at the back of the book, can serve as the shopping list.

Equipment, like effort, can be abbreviated. A toaster oven or broiler is particularly useful; we have ours on a shelf over the stove, duplicating the professionals' system for defrosting, holding cooked food, turning out stacks of toast, etc. Here is a rundown of appropriate utensils:

vegetable scrub brush
vegetable peeler
strainer/colander
box or drum grater
tongs
long-handled fork
metal spatula
ladle
citrus squeezer
tea strainer
sharp knives
vegetable steamer

scissors
egg slicer
cheese slicer
pot holders
small casserole or
    oven trays
several saucepans
    (1- to 5-quart capacity)
6- to 8-inch omelet pan
10- to 12-inch omelet pan
12- to 15-inch skillet
tea kettle

Other useful items include:

pressure cooker
wok
pan with nonstick finish
griddle
electric skillet
electric grain cooker

food processor
salad spinner
muffin tin
baking sheet
loaf pan
chef's apron

Preparation and Cooking Time

Preparation times vary depending on the proficiency of the cook, and cooking times may be affected by differences in burners and ovens, by the degree to which utensils conduct heat, and by the ratio of contents to capacity. Check five minutes ahead of schedule to make sure the food isn't already cooked and be prepared to wait five to ten minutes beyond the expected cooking time.

Plan ahead by preparing a volume of long-cooking foods in advance or making intentional "leftovers." Having a store of cooked beans, grains, hard-cooked eggs, and other similar versatile foods on hand will be useful for expediting the preparation of many recipes.

Protein Content: Recipe Ratings

"Major Protein" signifies that a particular dish is of good-quality protein, offering 15 grams or more per serving, or *what you would expect from any nourishing main dish.*

A "Minor Protein" is a dish that supplies good-quality protein, *but a single serving does not contain enough of this nutrient* to serve as the only protein-giving food at a meal. That is, in normal amounts, it provides fewer than 15 grams. To make a meal adequate in protein a Minor Protein should be served with another Minor Protein or a Protein Complement.

"Protein Complement" is reserved for dishes that contain some but not all of the protein-building elements the body requires for optimal nourishment. In other words, the quality of the protein is lacking. Such foods can be raised to Major Protein status by combining them with a Minor Protein or the appropriate complement, as indicated by the diagram on page 5.

Protein Complements

The chart below illustrates the foods that complement each other. To create a high-quality protein meal, simply follow the direction of the arrows, incorporating something at either end. It is especially useful when planning a meal with Protein Complement recipes; classify them according to their predominant ingredient.

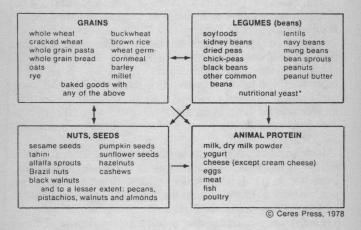

© Ceres Press, 1978

*Nutritional yeast has an amino acid pattern similar to legumes and thus can be combined with the same foods to enhance their protein value.

Seasoning

The most difficult place to be precise when writing a recipe is in the seasoning. Place of origin as well as growing, drying, and storing conditions can alter the potency of flavoring ingredients. Even more difficult to contend with is personal preference since each one of us has individually sensitive taste buds.

Thus you will probably want to adjust the seasoning in some recipes "to taste." Most professional chefs and experienced home cooks can rarely tell you how much of any herb or spice they use; they just taste and add, taste and add. The more home cooking you do, the easier seasoning will become. Until you feel comfortable about your own judgment, however, the recipe measurements will act as a good guideline.

The taste for salt, in particular, is largely adaptive. The main reason we give a salt measurement in recipes is that it is difficult to "salt to taste" a raw batter, uncooked soup or stew, and similar preparations that bear little relation to the final dish. Those accustomed to cooking with little or no salt may revise our guidelines. For those with a taste for more salty foods, we suggest following the recipe and then making salt and other flavor enhancers available at the table for those who need them. This will give your palate a chance to begin the process of savoring tastes other than salty.

Instead of adding salt, you can give foods a lift in cooking or at the table with fresh garlic, a dash of vinegar or fresh lemon juice, hot pepper sauce or fresh ground pepper, additional herbs and spices, ground kelp (a seaweed), or sesame salt (also called gomasio).

Unlike salt, we rarely give a measure for pepper. This is because we do all our "peppering" with a grinder, and it is a nuisance to grind and measure. Since pepper is best added at the last minute (it can turn bitter during cooking), it is no problem to add this seasoning "to taste."

Cooking Oils

The best oils for cooking are corn, peanut, soy, and in some special instances olive, since these oils withstand heat better than the lighter varieties such as sunflower and saf-flower. We use butter in cooking primarily for its taste. Where the choice of fat is subject to personal preference, it is listed in the ingredients as "oil/butter," which means either one or any combination.

For those who are insistent on eliminating fats in cooking, an equal amount of vegetable broth or water can generally replace the fat meant for sautéing, so that the food is braised instead. However, dishes prepared this way will lack some of their intended richness.

Milk

In the recipes, "milk" means you may use raw or pasteurized, whole or fat-reduced, or the equivalent in dry milk powder. Soy milk may be used if preferred. Any exceptions to this will be specifically indicated.

Buttermilk, sour milk (not a common item since pasteurization), and yogurt thinned with milk to buttermilk consistency may be used interchangeably in cooking. If you have only regular milk, it can be "soured" by adding 1 tablespoon of vinegar or lemon juice to 1 cup, minus 1 tablespoon of milk. Let this stand in a warm spot for 10 minutes to "clabber."

Eggs

Unless otherwise directed, use large eggs (average two ounces each). Use of smaller or larger eggs will slightly alter results, especially if the recipe calls for more than two eggs.

Recipes

MASTER RULE

Begin each recipe by reading it through completely. Gather all the ingredients and appropriate utensils at your work space. *Do as much measuring, peeling, chopping, etc., as is practical before beginning to combine ingredients.* Prepare pans and oven if necessary. You are now ready to assemble, mix, cook, and concentrate on any unfamiliar techniques—*mastering* the recipe.

Convenience Soups

Although nothing can equal the flavor of a slow-simmered soup, there are many excellent homemade soups that can be prepared in a matter of minutes.

TAMARI BROTH

A basic broth that you can use to create any one or a combination of variations.

8 scallions, minced
1 tablespoon oil
4 cups water
¼ cup soy sauce
½ teaspoon salt

Cook scallions in oil for 1 minute to soften. Add water, bring to a boil, and simmer for 10 minutes. Add soy sauce and salt and return to a boil.

Serves 4

Variations: For *Tamari Broth with Greens*, shred 4 outer leaves of romaine lettuce and add when water boils.

For *Tamari Broth with Tofu*, add 8 ounces sliced fresh or frozen tofu after water has simmered for 5 minutes. Add soy sauce and salt and simmer 10 minutes longer.

For *Tamari Broth with Grain*, divide ½ pound cooked noodles or 2 cups cooked rice into 4 serving bowls. Pour basic broth or a variation over the grain. Consume the grain with chopsticks and drink the broth left at the end.

INSTANT SOUP

This is a basic recipe that can vary depending on your pantry. Only the base itself is constant.

Base

2 cups water
¼ to ½ cup tomato juice, or 1 tablespoon tomato paste diluted in ¼ cup warm water, or 2 to 4 Tomato Cubes (see page 246)
1 to 2 tablespoons soy sauce
1 scallion, thinly sliced

Enrichment

Shredded lettuce or spinach
Grated carrot
Grated zucchini
Corn kernels
Any cooked vegetable or bean
Any cooked grain
Pasta
Couscous
Tofu

Seasoning

Vegetable bouillon (add initially)
Split clove garlic (add initially)
Pinch turmeric (add just before serving)
½ tablespoon nutritional yeast (add just before serving to thicken)
½ tablespoon oil (add just before serving for richness)
Sesame salt (add at table)

Combine all Base ingredients, varying the amount of tomato and soy sauce to taste. Bring to a boil and add any of the items listed under Enrichment. Cook for 5 minutes. If uncooked pasta is added, increase cooking to 10 to 15 minutes. Season with any of the Seasonings as directed in that list. If no grain is added, crumble whole grain crackers into the soup before eating.

Serves 2

PORTUGUESE BREAD AND GARLIC SOUP

This very substantial soup, made from the most modest ingredients, can be prepared in 10 minutes.

4½ cups water
4 cloves garlic, cut into pieces
1 teaspoon salt
4 to 6 slices (6 ounces) whole grain bread, torn into
  tiny pieces
pepper
parsley

Bring water to a boil. Add garlic, salt, and bread; simmer for 5 minutes, or until very soft. Mash with a spoon or fork. Return soup briefly to a boil. Season generously with fresh ground pepper, adjust salt if necessary to taste, and sprinkle with parsley.

Serves 4

Menu Suggestions: To make this into a Minor Protein, put ¼ cup or more of diced mozzarella, provolone, Swiss, or other stringy melting cheese in each bowl before adding hot soup; or top each bowl with ¼ cup of grated cheese.

EGG DROP SOUP

Add interest and substance to any broth with this simple technique.

3½ cups vegetable broth, liquid drained from
    canned tomatoes, or Tamari Broth (page 11)
2 teaspoons soy sauce (omit with Tamari Broth)
2 scallions, thinly sliced
1 egg, slightly beaten

Bring broth to a boil. Add soy sauce and scallions and simmer for 5 minutes. Just before serving, drizzle egg into simmering soup in a slow, steady stream. When egg "sets" or coagulates, give the soup a stir and serve.
Serves 4
Variation: For a slightly tart soup, add 1 tablespoon lemon juice to the broth initially.

CREAMED CORN SOUP

2 cups corn kernels
4 cups milk
¼ cup nonfat dry milk powder
1 thin slice onion
2 teaspoons salt
2 slices whole grain bread

Combine all ingredients in a blender or a processor fitted with a steel chopping blade. Process at high speed for about 30 seconds, or until corn is coarsely pureed. Pour into a saucepan and warm over moderate heat without boiling.
Serves 4 to 6
Major Protein

RAW ONION MILK SOUP

Quick, delicate, and as soothing as "milk toast."

1½ cups milk
¼ teaspoon salt
1 cup thinly sliced onion
about 1 teaspoon butter
paprika or nutmeg
crackers or croutons

Bring milk just to the boiling point and remove from heat. Add salt and onion and mash with a wooden spoon to extract onion flavor. Cover and let sit for a few minutes.

If soup has cooled, warm through, then strain liquid into serving bowls, add a little butter to each, and sprinkle surface with paprika or nutmeg. Serve with crushed crackers or croutons.

Serves 2

Minor Protein

Note: The remaining onions will be quite sweet and mild. Refrigerate and use on salads and sandwiches.

BLENDER SALAD SOUP

Similar to a classic gazpacho but with all the vegetables chopped right along with the tomato, making it much quicker to prepare.

4 medium-size ripe tomatoes
½ large green pepper
½ small onion
1 small cucumber
1 clove garlic
¼ teaspoon hot pepper sauce
1 teaspoon salt
2 tablespoons olive oil
3 tablespoons wine vinegar
½ cup ice water
6 ice cubes

Quarter tomatoes; seed and slice green pepper; peel and slice onion and cucumber; peel garlic.

Place vegetables and remaining ingredients except ice in a blender or a processor fitted with a steel blade and blend for about 3 seconds, until vegetables are finely chopped but not reduced to puree. Spoon soup into bowls and place an ice cube in each so it becomes very cold.

Serves 6

Note: If blender or processor cannot handle this quantity, process in batches.

QUICK MIXED VEGETABLE SOUP

A real "soup 'n' sandwich" soup.

2 medium carrots, cut up
2 stalks celery with leaves, cut up
½ cup onion pieces
several leafy greens or parsley sprigs
2 cups water
2 cups tomato juice
½ teaspoon salt
¼ teaspoon dried basil
1 teaspoon soy sauce
1 tablespoon oil or butter
pepper
1 tablespoon nutritional yeast (optional)

In a blender or processor fitted with a steel chopping blade combine vegetables and 1 cup water. Process to a thick puree.

Combine vegetable puree, remaining water, and tomato juice in a pot and bring to a boil. Add salt, basil, and soy sauce, and simmer for 5 minutes.

Remove from heat and stir in oil or butter, pepper to taste, and, if desired, the nutritional yeast, which will thicken the soup slightly.

Serves 4

Variations: For a more substantial soup, add ½ cup uncooked pasta, cracked wheat, or kasha along with the seasonings and simmer for 15 minutes, or until tender. Leftover cooked grain, beans, or vegetables can also be added.

QUICK TOMATO-ONION SOUP

A good appetizer or lunch soup that can be prepared in less than half an hour.

    2 tablespoons oil
    2 cups chopped onion
    3 cups vegetable broth or water
    2 cups tomato juice
    salt
    pepper
    1 teaspoon butter
    2 to 3 cups Cheese Croutons (recipe follows)

Put oil and onions in a saucepan and cook over low heat until onions begin to color lightly, about 10 minutes.

Add broth or water, cover, and simmer for 10 minutes. Stir in tomato juice and salt and pepper to taste. Bring to a boil. Stir in butter and, when melted, serve with Cheese Croutons (allow ½ cup per person).

Variation: Replace vegetable broth and tomato juice with 5 cups liquid drained from canned tomatoes

CHEESE CROUTONS

    whole grain bread
    finely grated Parmesan cheese
    oil (optional)

Preheat oven to 350°F. Cut bread into ¼-inch cubes. Mix with one fourth their volume Parmesan cheese (¼ cup cheese for each cup bread cubes).

Place in a well-buttered baking dish and bake for about 10 minutes, or until golden. Stir a few times during baking and drizzle with a little oil if desired.

Serve straight from the oven, or let cool to room temperature. Any cheese that adheres to the pan should be loosened and mixed with the croutons or sprinkled into the soup.

Minor Protein

Note: These can be used to garnish salads as well as soups.

QUICK CREAMY BEAN SOUP

An excellent outlet for cooked beans, either plain or in a seasoned sauce.

Combine cooked beans with an equal amount of milk, allowing 1 cup each for 2 small servings, 1½ cups each for a generous bowlful. Puree smooth in a blender or processor fitted with the steel chopping blade.

If beans are unseasoned, flavor as desired with salt, pepper, cumin, cayenne, or hot pepper sauce. Warm through and serve.

Major Protein

Note: Soup can be varied by using leftover cheese sauce instead of plain milk, or by adding grated cheese at the end and letting it melt in.

BROCCOLI AND MACARONI SOUP

1 tablespoon oil
1 small clove garlic, chopped
4 cups liquid drained from canned tomatoes, or
   water plus 2 tablespoons tomato paste
1 teaspoon salt (reduce it tomatoes are salted)
pepper
4 cups chopped broccoli
1 cup small whole wheat shells or macaroni
¼ cup grated Parmesan cheese

Heat oil in a 3-quart pot and sauté garlic until lightly colored. Add tomato liquid, salt, a generous grind of pepper, and bring to a boil.

Add broccoli; cover and simmer for 10 minutes. Add pasta, cover, and simmer 10 minutes longer, or until tender. Sprinkle with cheese and serve.

Serves 4
Minor Protein

WHITE GAZPACHO

This soup offers the alluring flavor of garlic that character-izes traditional gazpacho, but in a cucumber base. For those who object to garlic, it can be omitted and replaced with 2 tablespoons fresh dill. Serve this soup very cold with a choice of garnishes including croutons, diced tomato, chopped scallion, and chopped sweet red or green pepper.

2 cups peeled, diced cucumber
1 small clove garlic
½ cup parsley
½ teaspoon salt
2 tablespoons white vinegar
2 cups yogurt
½ cup sour cream

Combine cucumber, garlic, parsley, salt, and vinegar in a blender or processor fitted with a steel blade and blend smooth. Stir in yogurt and sour cream until evenly mixed. Chill before serving.

Makes 1 quart; serves 4

Minor Protein

Note: To make this soup without a blender or processor, grate cucumber fine on a cheese grater, mash garlic, chop parsley very fine, and mix all ingredients together.

MOROCCAN YOGURT SOUP

In this mellow soup the fresh mint works to counteract the aftereffects of the garlic.

2 cups yogurt
¼ cup coarsely chopped walnuts
1 cup peeled, shredded cucumber
1 small clove garlic, crushed
¼ cup chopped fresh mint
½ teaspoon salt
4 ice cubes

Beat yogurt with a wire whisk or fork until smooth. Stir in remaining ingredients except for the ice. Chill. Serve with an ice cube in each bowl.

Serves 4

Minor Protein

Variation: Some finely chopped pistachios sprinkled on top of each serving adds a glamorous touch.

Nibbles and Noshes

People who lead a fast-paced life or spend little time in the kitchen each day are less likely to sit down to three formal meals. More often they enjoy a practice which today is called "grazing" and was formerly known as "nibbling" or in some circles "noshing."

GUACAMOLE

The standard Mexican avocado "salad." Serve with tacos or mound on lettuce leaves on individual serving plates.

1 clove garlic
1 large or 2 small very ripe avocados
1 tablespoon lemon juice
1 small tomato, finely chopped
½ teaspoon salt
¼ teaspoon hot pepper sauce

Cut garlic in half and rub bowl well with cut surface. Discard. Cut avocado meat from peel and mash in serving bowl with fork. Add remaining ingredients. Serve immediately or place avocado pit in center, cover, and refrigerate before serving. (This will keep the avocado from turning brown.)
Serves 4

HUMMUS

A garlic-laced chick-pea puree. Serve with raw carrots, green pepper wedges, and cauliflowerets for dipping, as well as with the traditional pita bread.

2 cups cooked chick-peas
¼ cup bean liquid
¼ cup lemon juice
2 cloves garlic, finely minced
1 teaspoon salt (reduce if beans are well salted)
3 tablespoons tahini
2 tablespoons chopped parsley
2 tablespoons olive oil (optional)

Puree chick-peas in a processor or blender, adding the liquid for a smooth, creamy puree. Transfer to a shallow serving bowl and beat in lemon juice, garlic, and salt; then gradually add tahini to form a thick, light paste.

Let stand for about 30 minutes so flavor has a chance to develop. Sprinkle with parsley and, if desired, drizzle oil over surface just before serving.

Serves 4
Minor Protein

ONION DIP

This is a dip everyone is familiar with, but few realize it can be made a lot better—and for a lot less money—if you don't use a packaged soup mix.

1½ tablespoons instant minced onion
⅓ cup sour cream
⅔ cup yogurt
2 teaspoons dried parsley
good dash soy sauce

Combine all ingredients and let stand at least 20 minutes to develop flavor.
Makes 1 cup
Minor Protein

GREEN DIP

½ cup cottage cheese
½ cup yogurt
2 scallions, cut up
½ cup parsley, tightly packed
¼ teaspoon dry mustard
dash hot pepper sauce

Combine all ingredients in a blender and process until mixture is smooth and parsley is finely chopped.
Makes 1 cup
Minor Protein
Note: To prepare in a food processor, use the steel chopping blade and add only 2 tablespoons yogurt initially. Stir in remaining yogurt after processing.
Variations: Add 1 teaspoon fresh dill or 1 tablespoon fresh basil leaves.

PIMIENTO—CHEESE DIP

½ cup yogurt
2 whole pimientos, or 4-ounce jar, drained
1 teaspoon Dijon mustard
2 teaspoons soy sauce
1 cup (about 4 ounces) cheddar cheese, cut into
  small pieces

Puree yogurt, pimientos, mustard, and soy sauce in a blender or a processor with a steel chopping blade. With machine running, gradually feed in cheese. Puree until smooth. Stop machine and scrape dip from sides with rubber spatula as necessary.

Makes 1¼ cups
Minor Protein

BAKED BRIE WITH ALMONDS

A specialty of Mr. B's of New Orleans as reproduced in our kitchen.

8-ounce wheel Brie
2 tablespoons sliced almonds
½ tablespoon butter

Preheat oven or toaster oven to 325°F. Remove top layer of rind from cheese. Place in small oven-to-table baking dish. Spread almonds over exposed cheese. Dot with butter. Bake about 15 minutes until soft and runny. Serve at once.

Serves 4
Minor Protein
Note: To serve, scoop cheese out of rind onto serving plates with a spoon. Eat on crisp whole grain crackers. As

the cheese cools, it will become firm and the rind and remaining cheese can be cut into wedges and eaten with a fork.

Variation: For *Baked Camembert with Almonds*, replace Brie with Camembert. The wheels packed in tins available at supermarkets are perfectly adequate for this dish.

VEGETABLE COTTAGE CHEESE

This high-protein salad can be served on a bed of greens, in avocado shells, on a baked potato, on sliced tomatoes, or on crackers.

1 cup cottage cheese
1 cup mixed vegetables from the following, chopped
   as fine or coarse as you wish:

carrot	scallion
green pepper	cucumber
celery	tomato
radish	parsley

1 tablespoon cider vinegar or lemon juice
2 tablespoons yogurt, sour cream, or mayonnaise
½ teaspoon of one of the following:

paprika	dill
soy sauce	oregano
cumin	celery seed
caraway seeds	

2 dashes hot pepper sauce (optional)

Combine all ingredients to taste.
Serves 4
Minor Protein
Note: If portion sizes are doubled, this can serve as a Major Protein main course dish for lunch or a light supper.

OIL-CURED MOZZARELLA

Inspired by the Café des Artistes in New York City.

8 ounces mozzarella, cut into ¾-inch cubes
2 tablespoons olive oil
2 tablespoons light vegetable oil (sunflower or
    safflower)
2 teaspoons lemon juice
½ teaspoon dried crushed oregano
2 tablespoons chopped fresh parsley

Mix all ingredients and let stand for several hours to marinate. Serve at room temperature with a garnish of olives, tomato wedges, and capers.

Serves 6 to 8
Minor Protein
Note: Refrigerate in covered container for use within 2 weeks.
Menu Suggestions: This is a good choice as a first course preceding a pasta entrée.

TOMATO WITH CHÈVRE

Thick tomato slices with a topping of creamy French goat cheese and fresh basil.

4 medium to large tomatoes
4 ounces French goat cheese such as Montrachet
    or Boucheron
¼ cup chopped fresh basil

Cut each tomato into 3 thick slices. Arrange in a single layer in a shallow ovenproof pan. Cut cheese into small pieces and place evenly over tomato slices. Top with basil.

Broil for 3 to 5 minutes, until cheese is delicately browned. Serve at once.

Serves 4
Minor Protein

SAVORY SMOKY TOFU

This is quick and easy to prepare and can boost the food value of many Chinese vegetable dishes.

1 pound frozen tofu
2 tablespoons oil
4 scallions, sliced
2 tablespoons soy sauce

Reconstitute tofu in hot water as described on page 240. Press gently to expel water. Cut each piece into 4 squares.

Heat oil in a wok or skillet. Add scallion and cook for 1 minute. Add tofu and cook for 5 minutes, turning pieces as they begin to color.

Sprinkle tofu with soy sauce, stir quickly but gently and, when dry, remove from heat.

Serves 4
Minor Protein

STUFFED LEMON EGGS

Cold eggs with a light lemony filling.

6 hard-cooked eggs
¼ teaspoon finely minced lemon rind
1 tablespoon lemon juice
3 tablespoons yogurt
½ teaspoon salt
dash hot pepper sauce
12 capers

Peel eggs and halve lengthwise. Remove yolks and mash with lemon rind, juice, yogurt, salt, and hot pepper sauce. Adjust seasoning to taste.

Fill whites with yolk mixture. Top each half with a caper. If not served promptly, cover and refrigerate.

12 halves; serves 6
Minor Protein

CHEESE-STUFFED MUSHROOMS

16 medium to large mushrooms
½ cup creamed cottage cheese or ricotta cheese
¼ cup wheat germ
½ teaspoon salt
1 teaspoon oregano
pepper
paprika

Preheat oven or toaster oven to 400°F. Remove stems from mushrooms, clean and chop. Mix chopped mushroom stems with cottage cheese, wheat germ, salt, oregano, and pepper.

Clean caps and stuff with cheese filling. Place, filling side up, in a well-oiled baking dish; sprinkle liberally with paprika and bake for 10 minutes until hot and tender. Serve at once.

Serves 4
Minor Protein
Note: Mushrooms can be stuffed in advance and refrigerated until baking time.

COLD STUFFED TOMATO

Use this dish to add a little protein to a pasta or bean entrée.

2 medium tomatoes
1 slice whole grain bread
1 tablespoon wine vinegar
⅛ teaspoon salt
pepper
1 tablespoon minced parsley
1 teaspoon minced fresh basil or ½ teaspoon dried
2 tablespoons cottage cheese

Cut a thin slice from top of tomatoes and scoop out pulp, leaving a shell. Invert to drain. Save liquid for stock and dice pulp.

Dice bread and mix with tomato pulp, vinegar, salt, a generous amount of fresh pepper, and herbs. Let stand until well moistened (10 minutes is long enough but this can also be prepared hours in advance). Before serving, mix cottage cheese with bread filling and pack into tomato shells.

Serves 2
Minor Protein

MOZZARELLA-STUFFED TOMATO

Use this stuffed tomato as an accompaniment to pasta or grain entrées, or double the serving sizes and use on any plain pasta or grain dish instead of sauce.

    4 medium tomatoes
    salt
    1 cup finely diced mozzarella cheese
       (about 4 ounces)
    1 tablespoon chopped fresh basil or 1 teaspoon
       dried
    pepper
    olive oil

Cut tops from tomatoes and scoop out seeds and liquid with a small spoon. Leave pulp intact. Salt lightly and invert for 10 to 15 minutes to drain. Preheat oven or toaster oven to 350°F. Mix diced cheese with basil and pack into tomatoes. Season generously with pepper.

Place tomatoes close together in a baking dish well coated with olive oil. Drizzle a little oil in each tomato. Bake for about 15 minutes until tomato is hot and cheese melted.

Serves 4

Minor Protein; Major Protein when doubled

Note: This can be assembled in advance and baked before serving.

BROILER POTATO CRISPS

Crisp broiled potato slices can be served hot from the broiler or munched like potato chips with dips.

raw potatoes (allow 1 medium potato per serving)
oil
salt (optional)

Scrub potatoes and, if time permits, chill them. Slice into ⅛-inch-thick rounds using a knife or the slicing blade of a food processor. Place on an oiled baking sheet and brush with oil.

Broil about 3½ inches beneath heat for about 10 minutes until golden. Turn and broil 5 to 10 minutes longer. Check frequently to avoid overcooking. Some pieces will cook more quickly than others and should be removed when done. (Potatoes can also be "crisped" in a 450°F. oven for about 10 minutes.) Sprinkle lightly with salt, if desired, before serving.

Note: For individual servings, prepare in toaster oven. Potato Crisps can be seasoned at the table with a light sprinkling of vinegar instead of salt.

TOASTED NOODLES

A great snack, sandwich accompaniment, or crunchy noodles for Chinese food made from fresh-cooked or leftover spaghetti. It is easily done in the toaster oven or broiler.

whole wheat spaghetti, broken into 1-inch pieces
oil

Use leftover cooked spaghetti or cook spaghetti in boiling salted water until just tender, about 10 minutes. Drain well, cool under cold running water, and pat dry. When pasta is dry, coat lightly with oil, using 1 tablespoon per 2 cups spaghetti. Place on broiler tray and brown, stirring a few times so it cooks evenly. Best when served soon after cooking.

Makes 2 cups; serves 4
Protein Complement

DRY-ROASTED NUTS

Lightly roasting nuts and seeds brings out a rich, deep flavor.

unroasted nuts and/or seeds of choice

Add enough nuts and/or seeds to fit comfortably in an ungreased skillet and place over moderate heat. Roast until lightly browned, about 5 minutes. If pumpkin seeds are being roasted, watch (and listen) for them to swell and pop. Shake pan occasionally for even browning and monitor carefully as soon as they begin to color, as they darken all of a sudden.

Cool completely before storing in airtight containers.
Protein Complement
Variation: For *Soy-Roasted Nuts*, dilute 2 tablespoons
soy sauce with 1 teaspoon water for every ¾ cup nut/seed
mixture. Stir into dry-roasted nuts, standing away from pan
in case liquid spatters. Cook about 30 seconds until liquid
evaporates.

QUICK PICKLES

A crunchy pickle with a simple brine that can be replen-
ished so that there is always a fresh supply of pickles in the
refrigerator.

   2 unwaxed or peeled cucumbers
   1 small onion
   1 small clove garlic, minced
   1 tablespoon fresh dill, or 1½ teaspoons dill seed
   1 cup hot water
   2 tablespoons honey
   1 tablespoon salt
   3 tablespoons cider vinegar

Slice each cucumber lengthwise into 8 sticks. Slice onion
into rings. Alternate layers of cucumber and onion in a
broad nonmetal dish. Scatter garlic and dill on top.

Mix water with honey and salt to dissolve; add vinegar
and pour this brine over the cucumber. Cover and refrigerate for at least 6 hours before using.
Makes 16 pickles
Note: When ready to replenish the pickle container add
1 tablespoon vinegar and 1 rounded teaspoon honey to
the brine and add more sliced cucumbers and onion as
needed. Prepare a fresh solution after 2 or 3 batches have
been made.

GREEK OLIVES

Here is a simple but effective way to improve on bland canned black olives.

1 can (7¼ to 8 ounces drained weight) unpitted
    black olives
2 tablespoons wine vinegar
2 tablespoons olive oil
¼ teaspoon crushed dried oregano
1 clove garlic, sliced

Drain liquid from canned olives, reserving ½ cup. Combine reserved liquid with remaining ingredients and pour over olives in a bowl or jar. Cover and marinate in the refrigerator for 12 hours before use.

Note: These can be stored in the refrigerator for about 2 weeks.

MARINATED ARTICHOKE HEARTS

Brighten up canned artichokes with your own marinade.

15-ounce can artichoke hearts packed in water
2 tablespoons lemon juice
3 tablespoons oil (at least part olive preferred)
¾ teaspoon oregano
¼ teaspoon salt
pepper

Drain artichokes, rinse, and cut in quarters. Pour lemon juice and oil over artichokes. Add seasonings and mix well. Taste and adjust salt if necessary. Let stand at room temperature for use within several hours, or refrigerate. Stir occasionally for even marination.

Serves 4

PICKLED MUSHROOMS

1 pound mushrooms
1 cup red wine vinegar
½ cup water
8 peppercorns
1 bay leaf
1 teaspoon salt
2 cloves garlic, crushed with the flat blade of a
   knife
1 to 2 tablespoons oil

Clean mushrooms. Combine all ingredients except mushrooms and oil in a saucepan and bring to a boil. Add mushrooms and simmer for 2 minutes. Remove from heat and cool to room temperature.

Remove garlic and transfer mushrooms and broth to a jar. Slowly pour oil on top. Cover jar and chill for 24 hours before using.

Makes about 1 quart

Note: Can be stored for several weeks in the refrigerator.

MARINATED ZUCCHINI STICKS

These flavorful zucchini sticks can be served as a salad or a salad garnish.

2 medium zucchini (about 1 pound)
4 tablespoons wine vinegar
2 tablespoons oil
1 clove garlic, split
¼ teaspoon salt
pepper
1 teaspoon dried basil
1 tablespoon minced parsley

Trim ends of zucchini and cut into sticks 1½ inches long and 1½ inches wide. Combine remaining ingredients in a small saucepan and bring to a boil. Pour over zucchini and mix well.

Chill zucchini several hours, stirring occasionally so all pieces are marinated. To store, transfer to a covered jar.

Serves 4 to 6

Note: This dish should be prepared in advance. It keeps in the refrigerator about 5 days.

NACHOS

Nachos are crisp corn chips topped with melted cheese. Serve plain or with a dollop of hot Mexican sauce. They are a quick and handy accompaniment to rice-and-bean entrées and a good snack too.

  1 corn tostada or ¼ cup corn chips
  2 to 3 tablespoons shredded Jack cheese
  cumin
  canned chilies (optional)
  spicy Mexican sauce (optional) such as Quick
    Mexican Hot Sauce (page 170)

Place tostada or chips on a baking sheet or, for individual preparation, the tray of the toaster oven. Top with cheese and a light sprinkling of cumin. Arrange strips of chili pepper on top if desired.

Broil until cheese is bubbly. Serve with a little hot sauce spooned on top.

Minor Protein

PARMESAN TOAST

Good with Italian food and vegetable meals in need of a little boost.

  2 thin slices rye or whole wheat bread
  butter
  2 tablespoons grated Parmesan cheese (or Romano,
    locatelli, sardo, etc.)

Toast bread lightly and spread with a thin layer of butter. Top each slice with 1 tablespoon grated cheese. Broil or top-brown in toaster oven until bubbly.

Serves 1 to 2
Minor Protein

GARLIC—SESAME BREAD

A good accompaniment to Italian meals when a whole wheat Italian loaf is not available.

4 slices whole wheat bread
1½ tablespoons tahini
1½ tablespoons olive oil
1 small clove garlic, minced
pinch salt
sesame seeds

Toast bread lightly. Beat together tahini, oil, garlic, and salt. Spread liberally on toast. Sprinkle lightly with sesame seeds.

Broil or top-brown in toaster oven just before serving so that spread bubbles a bit; watch carefully so that seeds don't burn, and serve while hot.

Serves 2 to 4

Variation: For *Parsley—Sesame Bread*, replace garlic with 1 tablespoon dried parsley.

BREAD & SPREAD

This delicious, nourishing spread for bread replaces butter in many health-conscious kitchens.

½ cup tahini
1 tablespoon soy sauce
2 tablespoons lemon juice
about 1 tablespoon water
1 clove garlic, crushed
dill, cumin, parsley

Using a fork, beat together tahini, soy sauce, and lemon juice to make a thick paste. Beat in a little water to make a thick spread. Flavor with garlic and other herbs from those suggested here or use your favorites.

Makes ½ cup
Protein Complement
Note: Stored in the refrigerator, this will keep one week.

BREAD TURNOVERS WITH CHEESE

A convenient way to add protein to a soup, salad, or vegetable plate.

1 cup grated cheese
⅓ cup cottage cheese
¼ cup minced parsley
1 egg, lightly beaten
8 slices whole grain bread
milk

Combine cheeses, parsley and most of the egg to form a thick filling. Save a little of the egg for brushing the turnovers later on. Chill cheese mixture until ready to bake.

Preheat oven to 400° to 425°F.

Cut crusts from bread and roll flat in all directions. Place 1 tablespoon cheese filling on half and fold into a triangle. Press edges with a fork to seal. Place on an oiled baking sheet.

Beat reserved egg with a little milk and paint tops of turnovers.

Bake for 12 to 15 minutes until browned.

Makes 8 turnovers; serves 4 to 8
Minor Protein
Note: Filling mixture can be made well in advance but the actual assembly should be done just before baking.

Cold Sandwiches and Sandwich Fillings

Overstuffed sandwiches provide filling meals that are enjoyable and easy to assemble. Many are based on traditional luncheonette fare; others make clever use of vegetable proteins to create familiar textures and tastes. While the term "chicken salad" conjures up a definite image for most people, Chopped Bean Liver or Chick-Pea Salad may suffer from a lack of gustatory associations. However, despite their unglamorous names and basic ingredients, the sandwich fillings in this section make surprisingly good eating and are particularly valuable for the interest they can add to packed lunches. Moreover, many of them can be piled onto a bed of lettuce for salad platter entrées.

Note: Those recipes classified as "Minor Protein" or "Protein Complement" will achieve main dish status when served on whole grain bread.

CHEESON

Fried provolone cheese, which we call "Cheeson," resembles bacon to a remarkable degree. It even releases its own natural fat as it cooks, making the similarity more striking. In addition to being used in sandwiches, Cheeson can be crumbled onto salads or served with pancakes, eggs, or whenever you would welcome its salty-smoky taste and crisp texture. For best results, use high-quality aged provolone.

Place sliced provolone cheese in a well-seasoned skillet or pan with a nonstick finish over medium-high heat. Cook until bubbles appear and break on the surface and cheese begins to show color through the holes. (Keep in mind that cheese will continue to cook until removed from the pan. After a few times, you will recognize the proper degree of doneness.) For crisp rather than silky Cheeson, you can turn the cheese and cook the other side.

Remove from heat and let Cheeson sit in the pan a few minutes to harden. Lift from the pan. When cool, tear into strips about 1½ inches wide, or 3 per slice.

CLT

Combine Cheeson with the traditional ingredients for the American Wholefoods version of the classic BLT.

1½ slices (1½ ounces) Cheeson per sandwich
2 slices whole wheat toast
mayonnaise
lettuce
sliced tomato

Serves 1
Major Protein

C & C

The best of two worlds—the smoothness of cream cheese and the nourishment of cottage cheese.

2 slices whole grain bread, plain or toasted
2 tablespoons cream cheese
¼ cup cottage cheese

Spread cream cheese to cover one slice of bread. Add cottage cheese, a garnish from the list below, if desired, and top with second slice of bread.
Serves 1
Major Protein
Garnishes: Filling can be enhanced with sliced tomato, chopped olives, finely chopped nuts, sliced cucumber, sprouts, or other chopped or shredded vegetable. Can also be made sweet with sliced banana, crushed pineapple, fruit butter, a thin coating of honey, or fruit- or honey-sweetened preserves.

KIDNEY BEAN LUNCHEON SALAD

2 cups cooked kidney or pink beans, drained
½ cup chopped celery
¼ cup chopped green pepper
2 diced hard-cooked eggs
2 tablespoons mayonnaise
2 tablespoons yogurt
salt (omit if beans are salted)
pepper

Combine all ingredients, adding mayonnaise and yogurt to moisten; season to taste.
Serves 4
Minor Protein
Note: If you have any homemade pickle relish or other high-quality relish, add ¼ cup to bean mixture.

LIMA BEAN—EGG SALAD

2 cups cooked dried lima beans, drained
2 hard-cooked eggs
2 carrots
½ teaspoon prepared mustard
2 tablespoons yogurt
3 tablespoons mayonnaise

If large limas are used, chop coarsely with a knife; small limas can be left whole. Chop egg. Grate carrot finely. Combine all ingredients and mix well.

Makes 2¼ cups; serves 4 to 6
Minor Protein

CHICK-PEA SALAD

Surprisingly similar to tuna salad.

1 cup cooked chick-peas, drained
1 stalk celery, chopped
up to ¼ cup chopped raw onion
1 hard-cooked egg, chopped (optional)
1 generous tablespoon mayonnaise
dash prepared mustard
lemon wedge
salt
pepper

Grind chick-peas in a processor or food mill, or mince fine by hand. Combine with celery, onion, and egg, if desired; add mayonnaise and mustard. Squeeze in lemon juice (which will reduce the need for salt) and season to taste with salt and pepper.

Makes about ⅔ cup; serves 2
Minor Protein; Protein Complement without egg

TOFU "EGG" SALAD

The mild flavor of tofu is easily enhanced by a well-seasoned dressing. Fresh tofu has the texture of hard-cooked eggs and, conveniently, requires no cooking.

4 ounces tofu
1 to 2 tablespoons any combination chopped celery,
   chopped green pepper, chopped onion
mayonnaise
mustard, dill, curry powder to taste

Dice tofu as you would hard-cooked eggs for salad. Add chopped celery, green pepper, and/or onion to taste. Add enough mayonnaise to make the mixture creamy. Season with any or all of the seasonings above or others as desired.

Makes ½ cup; serves 1
Protein Complement

DEVILED TOFU

Mustard dominates this pungent spread.

8 ounces tofu
2 teaspoons prepared mustard
½ teaspoon soy sauce
⅛ teaspoon turmeric (for color)
¼ cup minced green pepper
¼ cup minced onion (optional)
salt
⅛ teaspoon paprika

Mash tofu with a fork until crumbly. Add all the remaining ingredients, except the paprika, and mix well. Sprinkle paprika on top.

Makes 1½ cups (enough for 3 sandwiches or hors d'oeuvres for 4 to 6)
Protein Complement

TOFU "CHICKEN" SALAD

Even more convenient than chicken salad since you don't have to cook the tofu first.

8 ounces frozen tofu
1 large stalk celery, chopped
about 3 tablespoons yogurt
about 2 tablespoons sour cream or mayonnaise
2 tablespoons minced parsley
dash soy sauce
salt

Unwrap tofu, place in a deep bowl, and cover with boiling water. Let stand 10 minutes to defrost, then press out moisture between your palms. If still frozen, repeat the process. Shred tofu with your fingers and combine with remaining ingredients, moistening and seasoning to taste.

Makes about 1⅓ cups (fills 4 sandwiches or serves 2 as a salad)
Minor Protein
Variations: Adaptable to any chicken salad recipe; for example, replace parsley with 1 tablespoon fresh dillweed or add diced pineapple or walnuts to the mixture.

ANTIPASTO HEROES

Once you have the good Italian bread essential to an antipasto hero, your pantry and imagination are the only limitations. Here we pay tribute to New York's Trinacria, which became a legend with their salad in a sandwich.

For each serving:

1 6- to 8-inch hero roll or ¼ large whole wheat
    Italian bread
about ½ tablespoon olive oil
about 1 teaspoon vinegar
1 clove garlic, split (optional)
¼ cup finely shredded greens
1½ to 2 ounces sliced provolone cheese
several slices steamed potato
3 half-slices tomato
several Marinated Artichoke Hearts (page 36)
pimientos
capers
hot pickled peppers (or other pickled vegetable)
sliced olives
grated Parmesan cheese
about ½ teaspoon mustard
oregano
crushed red pepper

Split the roll or bread. (If very "bready," remove some of the soft interior and save for crumbs or the birds.) Spread bottom half with oil and vinegar. If desired, rub with cut edge of garlic.

Layer greens on bread. Top with cheese, a layer of potato, tomato, and artichoke; add pimiento strips, capers, pickled vegetable, olives, and grated Parmesan, as desired. (This list of condiments can be varied as you choose.)

Spread inside top half of roll or bread with mustard. Sprinkle with a little oregano and crushed red pepper. When you close the sandwich, press both halves together firmly to help keep the ingredients from falling out as you eat (this is really inevitable and part of the fun) and to improve the chances that it will fit in your mouth.

Serves 1

Major Protein

Note: If you are going to prepare heroes for 4, you will need to steam a large 6- to 8-ounce potato and prepare a full recipe of Marinated Artichoke Hearts. In addition, you will need 1 large tomato, 1 cup shredded greens, and 6 ounces provolone.

CHOPPED BEAN LIVER

A savory sandwich spread on the order of chopped liver.

> 1 cup cooked white beans or soybeans, drained
> 1 medium onion, chopped
> 1 tablespoon oil
> 1 teaspoon nutritional yeast
> salt
> pepper
> soy sauce (optional)

Grind beans in a processor or food mill or mince until fine. Sauté onion in oil until well browned. Mix beans, onion, and yeast, and season to taste. If desired, add soy sauce to darken to a liverlike color. Serve on bread or crackers, or mound onto a salad plate.

Makes about ⅔ cup; serves 2

Minor Protein

Note: A mashed hard-cooked egg can be added for improved protein value. If the recipe is doubled, still use only 1 egg.

OLIVE—BEAN SALAD

1 cup cooked soybeans, drained
¼ cup chopped green olives
1 generous tablespoon mayonnaise
1 teaspoon nutritional yeast

Grind beans in a processor or food mill or mince fine by hand. Combine with remaining ingredients and mix well.

Makes about ⅔ cup; serves 2
Minor Protein
Variation: Chopped sweet pickle or relish can also be added or used in place of the olives.

SESAME—BEAN PÂTÉ

1 cup cooked beans, drained
¼ cup tahini
about 2 teaspoons soy sauce
1 to 2 tablespoons any combination minced celery,
    green pepper, onion, scallion, parsley
1 clove garlic, minced

Grind beans, or mash with a fork if they are soft. Mix in tahini to form a thick, smooth paste and season with soy sauce, adjusting the amount according to the saltiness of the beans. Add any combination of the remaining ingredients you wish.

Makes about 1 cup (enough for 4 sandwiches)
Minor Protein

TOMATO—BEAN PÂTÉ

1 cup cooked red or pink beans (pinto,
   kidney, etc.), drained
2 to 3 tablespoons peanut butter
2 to 3 tablespoons tomato paste

Mash cooked beans with a fork. Add remaining ingredients to taste and mix until smooth.
Makes 1 cup (enough for crackers for 6, or 4 sandwiches)
Minor Protein

TEMPEH SANDWICH SALAD

¾ pound tempeh
about ⅓ cup mayonnaise
about ¼ cup yogurt
2 stalks celery, chopped
2 teaspoons prepared mustard
salt
pepper

Steam tempeh in a vegetable steamer for 15 minutes, then cool to room temperature. Cut into small dice. Mix with remaining ingredients, seasoning to taste.
Serves 4
Major Protein
Variation: Add onion, green pepper, chopped pickles or relish, walnuts, apple, parsley, or herbs

MILD CHEESE AND TOMATO SPREAD

1 cup (4 ounces) shredded cheddar cheese
6 tablespoons ricotta cheese
1½ tablespoons tomato paste
¼ to ½ teaspoon hot pepper sauce

Mash first 3 ingredients together until smooth; add hot pepper sauce to taste.

Makes 1 cup (enough for 4 sandwiches)

Minor Protein

OLIVE AND PIMIENTO CHEESE SPREAD

1 cup (4 ounces) shredded cheddar or Jack cheese
2 tablespoons chopped pimientos and green olives
(or use pimiento-stuffed olives)
½ teaspoon prepared mustard
¼ cup ricotta or small-curd cottage cheese

Combine all ingredients, mashing with a fork to a smooth, spreadable consistency.

Makes 1 cup (enough for 4 sandwiches)

Minor Protein

Variation: Shape into a brick 3 × 2 × 2 inches. Chill. Cut into 8 slices and serve on a bed of lettuce. Top with a dollop of mayonnaise.

CELERY CHEDDAR SPREAD

1 cup (4 ounces) shredded cheddar cheese
¼ cup finely chopped celery
2 tablespoons mayonnaise

Combine all ingredients, mashing with a fork to form a uniform paste.

Makes 1 cup (enough for 4 sandwiches)
Minor Protein

PROTEIN SPREAD

This simple spread is a good base for a variety of flavors.

1 cup cottage cheese
½ cup tahini
seasoning of choice: dill, cumin, caraway seeds, or
    other herbs
salt

Mash cottage cheese and tahini together until evenly blended. Flavor to taste with herbs of choice and salt.

Makes about 1¼ cups
Minor Protein

PEANUT BUTTER COMPLEMENTS

These peanut butter combinations offer the best taste and high-quality protein.

Peanut–Sesame Butter

4 parts peanut butter : 1 part tahini (sesame butter)

Peanut–Sunflower Crunch

2 parts peanut butter : 1 part chopped sunflower seeds

Creamy Peanut Butter

Add 1 tablespoon yogurt to each 4 tablespoons plain peanut butter or to any of the complemented spreads above

Minor Protein
Note: To save time, peanut butter can be premixed with tahini or sunflower seeds and stored in the refrigerator.

Hot Sandwiches

Many recipes in this section that call for broiling or baking are most efficiently done for one or two in a toaster oven.

FRESH TOMATO PITA PIZZA

A variation on the now classic English muffin pizza.

1 whole wheat pita bread
4 tomato slices or ¼ cup of Italian-style tomato
   sauce (15-Minute Italian Tomato Sauce, page
   171, or other sauce of choice)
½ cup shredded mozzarella cheese mixed with
   Parmesan to taste
sliced fresh mushrooms, olives, sweet peppers,
   onion (optional)
pinch of oregano
oil

Preheat the oven or toaster oven to 375°F. Separate pita bread into 2 rounds by piercing around circumference with the tines of a fork and gently prying apart. Place on baking sheet. Cover each round of bread with tomato slices or spread with sauce. Top with cheese and any of the optional ingredients you wish. Season with oregano and drizzle with a little oil. Bake for 10 minutes.
Serves 1
Major Protein

QUICK CALZONE

A creamy ricotta filling warmed inside pita bread pockets makes a quick substitute for the classic version of calzone.

¾ cup ricotta cheese
½ cup shredded mozzarella cheese
¼ cup shredded provolone cheese
¼ teaspoon oregano
salt
pepper
½ medium tomato, chopped and drained
2 whole wheat pita breads
pickled peppers or canned chilies (optional)

Preheat oven or toaster oven to 375°F. Mix cheeses and oregano thoroughly. Add salt and pepper to taste. Gently fold in tomato.

Cut each bread in half to form two pockets. Open carefully and stuff each half with about ⅓ cup cheese filling. Insert a few thin slices of pepper or chilies into each, if desired.

Place in a baking dish with cut side tilted up so filling doesn't ooze out. Bake for 10 to 15 minutes until cheese is melted and very hot.

Serves 2
Major Protein

INDIVIDUAL BEAN PIZZAS

1 cup cooked chick-peas or kidney beans, drained
1 small onion, minced
¼ cup minced green pepper
1 small clove garlic, minced
½ teaspoon oregano
¼ teaspoon dried basil
¼ cup tomato juice
salt (omit if beans are salted)
2 whole wheat pita breads
½ cup shredded mozzarella or provolone cheese
1 tablespoon oil
crushed red pepper (optional)

Preheat oven or toaster oven to 450°F. Grind beans in a food mill or processor, mince fine by hand, or mash with a fork if very soft. Mix with onion, green pepper, garlic, herbs, and tomato juice until nicely moistened. Add salt only if necessary.

Cut each pita bread in two flat circles by punching with tines of fork around circumference and gently prying apart. Spread bean mixture to cover surface of rounds, using about ¼ cup for each. Cover with cheese and drizzle with oil. Top with crushed red pepper, if desired (or serve red pepper at the table).

Place on a baking sheet and bake for 10 minutes until very hot and cheese is lightly colored.

Serves 2
Major Protein
Note: Serves 4 as an accompaniment to light pasta dishes.

FRENCH-TOASTED CHEESE SANDWICH

1 to 2 ounces sliced cheese
2 slices whole grain bread
1 egg
2 tablespoons milk
¼ teaspoon dry mustard
pinch salt
butter/oil

Sandwich cheese between slices of bread. Beat egg with milk, mustard, and salt. Soak sandwich in egg mixture on each side until all egg is absorbed.

Add butter alone or with oil to cover surface of skillet; heat. Sauté sandwich 3 to 5 minutes on each side until browned.

Serves 1
Major Protein

SOUFFLÉED CHEESE SANDWICH

An embellished open-face cheese sandwich that is tasty, easy, light, novel, and a perfect example of how to make something fancy out of simple, everyday ingredients.

1 egg, separated
pinch dry mustard
dash hot pepper sauce
⅓ cup shredded cheese
salt
2 slices whole grain bread
butter

Preheat oven or toaster oven to 350°F. Beat egg yolk with mustard and hot pepper sauce until light. Mix in cheese. Beat egg white until stiff, adding a pinch of salt when foamy. Fold into yolk mixture.

Toast bread on one side in broiler or toaster oven. Lightly butter untoasted sides and cover with cheese mixture. Place on baking sheet and bake for 10 to 12 minutes until puffed and set.

Serves 1

Major Protein

Note: A half serving, or one slice of bread with soufflé topping, is an excellent Minor Protein accompaniment for soups, salads, bean casseroles, vegetable dishes, and other light meals.

AVOCADO—CHEESE MELT

Dedicated to the spirit of the Joyous Lake.

1 slice whole grain bread per sandwich
ricotta or cottage cheese
avocado
salt
lemon juice
1 to 2 ounces sliced Jack, cheddar, or Swiss cheese
sesame or sunflower seeds

Cover bread with a thin layer of ricotta or cottage cheese. Top with avocado that has been mashed and lightly seasoned with salt and lemon juice. Add sliced cheese, sprinkle with seeds, and place under broiler or in toaster oven until cheese is melted.

Serves 1

Major Protein

VEGGIE REUBEN

An open-face melted cheese sandwich that gets a lift from the crunchy, flavorful coleslaw beneath the cheese.

1 oversize or 2 average slices whole grain bread
Revisionist Dressing (page 161)
⅓ to ½ cup Tangy Coleslaw (page 150) or your
    favorite recipe
2 tomato slices, cut in half
1½ to 2 ounces sliced Swiss, Muenster, cheddar,
    or colby cheese

Preheat oven or toaster oven to 350°F. Spread bread with dressing. Arrange coleslaw on top to cover, then add tomato slices and cheese. Bake about 10 minutes until cheese melts.

Serves 1
Major Protein
Note: If desired, add sliced raw onion, pickle relish, or bread-and-butter pickles.

GRILLED OPEN-FACE TOFU SANDWICH

1 small cake tofu (4 ounces)
2 slices whole grain bread
butter
prepared mustard
soy sauce
tomato slice (optional)
mayonnaise (optional)

Slice tofu into 4 thin pieces and press with absorbent paper to remove excess moisture. Toast bread lightly and spread with butter and a thin layer of mustard. Top with tofu and season lightly with soy sauce; add a slice of tomato, if desired. Broil until tofu is lightly browned. Serve hot with a dollop of mayonnaise on top, if desired, for extra flavor.

Serves 1
Major Protein

TOFU PITA

1 whole wheat pita bread
tahini
soy sauce
4 ounces tofu, thinly sliced
2 to 3 thin tomato slices
alfalfa sprouts
mayonnaise

Preheat oven or toaster oven to 350°F. Separate pita bread into two rounds by piercing around the circumference with a fork and gently prying apart. Season tahini with soy sauce to taste and spread generously on one pita round. Layer sliced tofu on top of tahini. Cover with tomato slices and bake about 10 minutes, until hot. Arrange sprouts over tofu and tomato. Spread remaining pita round lightly with mayonnaise and close sandwich.

Serves 1
Major Protein
Variation: For *Tempeh Pita*, replace tofu with thinly sliced tempeh that has been pan-fried. Baking is not needed in this version; however, you may wish to warm the pita bread before filling it.

PEPPER AND EGG HERO

Like its cold counterpart, the hot Hero (known also as a Sub, Grinder, Poor Boy, Hoagie, and Torpedo) knows no limits except a good bread and some inventiveness. Herewith, a favorite filling.

1 tablespoon butter/oil
½ large green pepper, cut into strips
3 eggs
salt
pepper
2 individual hero rolls or half a large
   whole wheat Italian bread

Heat fat in a 10- to 20-inch skillet; sauté pepper 5 minutes, or until tender. Beat eggs and season with salt and pepper. Pour over softened green pepper and when eggs begin to set, stir gently to break up the omelet. Cook to taste. Cut bread as for a sandwich, and fill with pepper and eggs.

Serves 2
Major Protein
Note: Grated Parmesan makes a nice seasoning for the egg mixture.

TEMPEH BURGERS

An easy way to begin with this intriguing food.

4 ounces tempeh
oil

Cut tempeh into burger-size squares. Heat oil to cover surface of skillet and, when hot, add tempeh squares. Cook about 5 minutes, or until bottom is golden.

Carefully add a few tablespoons of water to the pan, standing back so the spattering of water as it turns to steam does not burn you. Cover pan and steam tempeh a minute. Repeat process.

Turn tempeh, add a little oil to pan if necessary, and brown. Repeat steaming process two more times to soften.

Makes 2 burgers; serves 1

Major Protein

Menu Suggestions: Serve on a plate or bun with your favorite relish, catsup, lettuce, and tomato. Try Broiler Potato Crisps (page 33) on the side.

Hot Entrées

The main course, or entrée, is determined primarily by its designation as the focal point of the meal. It is generally the dish consumed in greatest quantity. We tend to think of the main course as the principal source of protein, but this need not be the case if this nutrient is adequately provided by other components of the meal, such as the appetizer, soup, salad, or some accompaniment.

You may find that your meals occasionally lack a main dish, being composed instead of several smaller dishes that add up to good nourishment. You may even prepare small servings of more than one main dish in order to have a well-endowed meal of greater variety.

MEXICAN PIZZA

Italian fast food with Mexican ingredients.

2 corn tortillas
¼ cup Emergency Mexican Tomato Sauce (page 170) or similar sauce
¼ cup combined shredded cheddar and Jack cheeses
several canned chili strips
a scant teaspoon oil

Preheat oven or toaster oven to 375°F. Place tortillas on a baking sheet and spread with sauce, cheese, and chili strips; drizzle lightly with oil. Bake for 10 minutes.
Serves 1
Major Protein

BEAN TACOS

Bean tacos are valued for their simplicity and festive quality.

3 taco shells
¾ cup Refried Beans (page 143)
chopped tomato
chopped raw onion
chopped green pepper
chopped cucumber
shredded lettuce
¼ cup or more shredded Jack or cheddar cheese
¼ cup or more Emergency Mexican Tomato Sauce
  at room temperature (page 170)
Quick Mexican Hot Sauce (optional, page 170)

Stuff each taco with ¼ cup beans, garnish to taste with vegetables, sprinkle with a generous spoonful of cheese, and smother with tomato sauce. Season with hot sauce to taste, if desired.

Serves 1

Major Protein

Note: If serving a group, bring all the ingredients to the table and let people assemble their own tacos.

Variation: For *Chalupas,* replace tacos with corn tortillas, allowing 2 per person and fry one at a time in enough heated oil to generously cover a skillet. Top each flat, crisp tortilla with the above ingredients, adding a layer of guacamole and a topping of yogurt flavored with sour cream to taste.

Menu Suggestions: Serve as a complete meal with Guacamole (page 23) or raw vegetables and a favorite dip, or combine on the menu with Cheese Enchiladas or Chili Rellenos (pages 69 and 68) as a double entrée.

TORTILLA PYRAMID

A stack of tortillas layered with cheese and topped with an egg is a more filling dish than you might expect, and as easy to make for many as for one.

3 corn tortillas
½ cup shredded Jack or cheddar cheese
1 tablespoon chopped olives
1 egg
oil
about ¼ cup Quick Mexican Hot Sauce (page 170)
    or chopped raw onions and tomatos flavored
    with hot pepper sauce

Toast each tortilla lightly in toaster oven, toaster, broiler, or by toasting over an open flame (using long-handled tongs). Stack on a baking pan with grated cheese and chopped olives between each layer.

Preheat oven or toaster oven to 375°F. Fry egg in oil until white is set but yolk is still soft. Place on top of tortillas, drizzle with a little oil, and bake for 5 to 10 minutes, just to melt cheese.

Season at the table with one of the recommended sauces.
Serves 1
Major Protein

BROCCOLI TOSTADOS

Vegetable-topped tortillas in a bean–cheese sauce.

½ pound broccoli, chopped (about 2 cups)
4 corn tortillas
Bean–Cheese Sauce (recipe follows)

Steam broccoli about 10 minutes until barely tender. Toast tortillas lightly in toaster or toaster oven set on "light," in broiler, or in an ungreased skillet. Pile broccoli on top of tortillas and cover with a generous amount of sauce.

Bean–Cheese Sauce

¾ cup cooked pinto or kidney beans, drained
⅓ cup milk
¾ cup diced cheddar or Jack cheese
¼ teaspoon salt (adjust if beans are salted)
¼ teaspoon hot pepper sauce

Combine all ingredients in blender or processor fitted with steel blade and puree until smooth. Transfer to a pot and heat gently until cheese melts and sauce is warm.
Serves 2
Major Protein

CHILI RELLENOS

Mexican batter-fried, cheese-stuffed peppers.

2 4-ounce cans whole green chilies
3 to 4 ounces Jack cheese
1 egg, separated
pinch salt
1 tablespoon cornmeal
oil/butter

Gently remove chilies from can and pat dry.

Cut cheese into thin sticks and slide into peppers until well stuffed.

Beat egg white until stiff peaks form. Beat in salt and yolk until evenly mixed. Fold in cornmeal.

Heat enough oil and/or butter to generously cover a large, heavy skillet. When hot, dip chilies, one at a time, into egg batter to coat (use tongs or your hands to hold them) and slip into hot fat. Cook until just set and golden on both sides, about 5 minutes. Serve plain or with any raw or cooked Mexican tomato sauce.

Serves 2 generously (3 as one of several entrées in a Mexican dinner)

Major Protein (When served for 3, at least one of the other dishes should include some protein.)

CHEESE RAREBIT

Rich cheese sauce over bread makes a delicious and warming meal. Serve pickles on the side for contrast.

4 slices whole grain bread
¾ cup Double Cheese Sauce (page 173)

Toast bread (do not butter it) and let sit at room temperature until sauce is made. (Day-old bread, rather than fresh, is actually better for this dish, and leftover toast from early in the day can be used as long as it is unbuttered.) Place 2 slices of bread on each serving plate and drown in sauce.

Serves 2
Major Protein

CHEESE ENCHILADAS

The Mexican crepe.

3 cups shredded Jack cheese alone or combined with cheddar
⅓ cup yogurt
½ cup chopped onion
2 cups Emergency Mexican Tomato Sauce (page 170)
12 corn tortillas

Preheat oven to 350°F.

Mix cheese, yogurt, and onion until evenly combined.

Heat tomato sauce to boiling and, holding a tortilla with tongs, dip into sauce briefly until pliable. Place 2 rounded tablespoons cheese filling in a strip along the center and roll tortilla to completely cover. Place seam-side down in a large, shallow, oiled baking pan.

Continue with each tortilla, placing them side by side in the pan, but not on top of one another. (If desired, casserole can be refrigerated at this time for cooking later.)

When ready to cook, spoon remaining sauce over filled tortillas and bake for about 10 minutes, or until cheese melts and sauce is bubbly. (If chilled, increase cooking time to 15 or 20 minutes.)

Serves 4 (or 6 at a larger meal as one of several entrées)
Major Protein

Note: Leftovers can be refrigerated or frozen. Frozen enchiladas should be reheated covered in a 375°F. oven for about 30 minutes, or until cheese melts and sauce bubbles.

POTATO PANCAKES

As easy to make as an omelet.

about 1 pound raw unpeeled potatoes (to make
   2 cups shredded)
1 small onion, grated
1 egg, lightly beaten
½ teaspoon salt
1 tablespoon wheat germ
about 1 tablespoon whole wheat flour
oil
Whipped Cottage Cream (page 164)

Shred potatoes coarsely using the shredding disk of a
food processor, or a box grater. If desired, grate a portion
more finely to make centers of pancakes chewy. Drain all
liquid from potatoes by pressing in a strainer. Mix remaining ingredients except Whipped Cottage Cream into drained
potatoes. If liquid or very loose, add more flour or some
whole wheat cracker crumbs.

Cover surface of large, heavy skillet with oil. When oil is
hot, drop potato mixture by soupspoonfuls into the pan.
Cook until brown underneath and easily turned, 5 to 8
minutes. Turn and brown the other side. Serve with Whipped
Cottage Cream.

Makes about 10 pancakes; serves 2

Major Protein (with topping)

Note: If you are cooking potato pancakes for a family or
a crowd, keep the first batches warm in a 300°F. oven
while you are cooking the rest.

Menu Suggestion: Potato pancakes are traditionally served
with applesauce and sour cream. However, to make them
an appropriate main dish, Whipped Cottage Cream is the
topping of choice.

CRISP CHEESE PANCAKES

Serve these savory pancakes as a hot entrée or cold sand-wich filling.

1 cup shredded cheese
2 tablespoons whole wheat flour
¼ teaspoon salt (less with a salted cheese)
1 teaspoon prepared mustard
2 eggs, lightly beaten
¼ cup yogurt
oil

Combine all ingredients except oil to make a uniform batter. Cover the surface of a griddle or skillet with oil and heat. When hot, drop batter by tablespoonfuls into the pan. Cook until brown underneath and easily moved with a spatula, 5 to 8 minutes. Turn and brown about 3 minutes on the other side.

Serves 2 generously as an entrée (4 as a sandwich filling)
Major Protein
Note: If you are making a number of pancakes, keep the ones that have been cooked warm in a 250° to 300°F. oven or toaster oven.

RICE PANCAKES

Although we originally designed this dish for breakfast, most people find these pancakes best for a quick lunch or dinner entrée. Crisp on the surface and tender inside, they need no embellishments, although catsup or a light yogurt–mayonnaise mixture can be used for seasoning.

1 cup cooked brown rice
1 egg
½ cup milk
½ cup diced Muenster or Jack cheese
oil

Combine, rice, egg, and milk in a blender or a processor fitted with a steel blade and process to combine. Add cheese and puree until evenly blended but still lumpy.

Heat enough oil to just cover the surface of a heavy skillet or griddle. Pour on batter, allowing ¼ cup per pancake. When edges become crisp and a spatula can easily be slid underneath, flip and cook until the bottom sets.

Makes 10 pancakes; serves 2
Major Protein
Note: Unless you have a very large griddle, you may need two pans. If you cook pancakes in separate batches, keep them warm in a 300°F. oven.

COTTAGE CHEESE CUTLETS

A quick and especially satisfying cutlet. Serve plain, Italian style with tomato sauce and grated Parmesan cheese, or Russian style with a topping of yogurt and fresh dill.

1 egg
1 slice whole grain bread
1 cup dry-curd pot cheese, or well-drained cottage
    cheese
¼ teaspoon salt
1 tablespoon minced parsley
¼ cup whole wheat flour
oil

Beat egg, then shred bread into beaten egg and let stand a few minutes to absorb. Add cottage cheese, salt, parsley, and 2 tablespoons of flour to the egg mixture. Stir until smooth.

Put remaining flour on a plate; taking ¼ cup of the cottage cheese mixture at a time, shape into 2-inch rounds and dredge with flour. Batter will be fairly soft but should hold together nicely.

Cover surface of a 15-inch skillet with oil and heat. When hot, fry cheese cutlets on each side until brown, or about 5 minutes per side. Serve plain or with any of the toppings described above.

Makes 4 cutlets; serves 2

Major Protein

Note: To drain cottage cheese, place in a strainer lined with a linen napkin or cheesecloth and let stand while assembling ingredients. Gather cloth around cheese like a bag and squeeze to extract as much liquid as possible.

SCRAMBLED EGGS WITH TOMATOES

1 tablespoon butter
2 scallions, thinly sliced
1 medium tomato, diced
½ tablespoon chopped fresh basil
4 eggs
salt
pepper
6 sliced olives (optional)
grated Swiss cheese

Melt butter in a 10- to 12-inch skillet and sauté scallions until softened, about 2 minutes.

Drain any liquid that has accumulated around the tomato and add the pulp to the skillet along with the basil. Cook until most of the moisture evaporates, about 5 minutes.

Beat eggs with a pinch of salt and generous turn of the pepper mill. Pour into the skillet and cook as for scrambled eggs, stirring as they begin to set, until they reach the desired degree of doneness.

Just before serving, stir in olives, if desired. Top with grated cheese.

Serves 2

Major Protein

Note: If the recipe is multiplied by two or three, it can be prepared in a 12- to 15-inch skillet.

GREEK BEANS, EGGS, AND CHEESE

1 tablespoon oil
2 tablespoons chopped scallion
¾ cup cooked chick-peas or white beans, drained
4 eggs
¼ teaspoon oregano
2 tablespoons minced fresh parsley
⅓ cup feta cheese
pepper

Heat oil in a 10- to 12-inch skillet and sauté scallions until they soften slightly. Stir in beans.

Beat eggs with oregano and parsley and pour over beans. As eggs begin to set, stir as for scrambled eggs. When set but still soft, add feta cheese in small cubes. Cook to desired consistency (loose or tight).

Season generously with pepper; reserve salt for seasoning at the table as needed.

Serves 2

Major Protein

Variations: For *Italian Beans, Eggs, and Cheese*, replace feta with ½ cup diced mozzarella, provolone, or a combination of these two cheeses. Serve with tomato and grated Parmesan cheese.

For *Mexican Beans, Eggs, and Cheese*, replace chick-peas with cooked kidney or pinto beans. Use ½ cup diced Jack cheese instead of feta and season scallions in skillet with ⅛ teaspoon chili powder before adding beans.

Menu Suggestions: For a Greek meal, add pita bread, sliced fresh tomato, olives, and plain yogurt or yogurt seasoned with cucumber and mint. The Italian counterpart will include Italian bread, olives, a salad of tomatoes and mixed greens, and for big eaters, a side dish of pasta. For a Mexican meal, serve with corn tortillas or crisp tacos, shredded greens, and any raw or cooked Mexican tomato sauce (page 170) for seasoning eggs.

CAMELLIA GRILL OMELET

A treasured eating spot in New Orleans is the Camellia Grill, and it is there we first had the omelet that inspired this hybrid of tender pancake with egg.

1 egg
¼ cup milk
⅛ teaspoon salt
2 tablespoons whole wheat flour
butter

Beat all the ingredients together using an egg beater, wire whisk, or blender. (At the Camellia they use a malted mixer.) Place a 15-inch skillet over medium heat. Rub the surface with a little butter to just coat.

When pan is hot, pour egg mixture in and let it spread as thin as possible. Cook until top is set but not dry and egg can be lifted with ease from the pan. (Lift the edge and check the color; it should be golden.) Fold the omelet by bringing two sides to the middle, then folding in the other two sides to form a neat package. Serve hot from the pan.

Serves 1

Minor Protein

Variations: Camellia Grill Omelets filled with ¼ to ½ cup shredded cheddar cheese or ½ cup chili, as is popular at the Louisiana diner, are especially recommended and are a *Major Protein* dish. Set the filling in the center of the large "pancake" just before folding and enclose in the bundle.

OMELET FINES HERBES

Egg chefs recommend making additional omelets for more than two servings rather than increasing the size of the omelet.

4 eggs
2 tablespoons chopped parsley
1 tablespoon chopped chives
½ teaspoon dried chervil or 2 teaspoons minced
    fresh, if available
pinch salt
1 tablespoon butter
grated Swiss and/or Parmesan cheese (optional)

Beat eggs with seasonings.

Melt butter in a 10-inch omelet pan. Pour in eggs and cook until bottom is set. Loosen at edges and lift egg away from the pan while you tilt it to allow any unset egg on top to run down the sides and underneath.

When set but still slightly soft on top, fold the omelet in half, or roll in thirds and transfer to a serving plate. Sprinkle cheese on top if desired.

Serves 2
Major Protein

MANICOTTI OMELET

If you like manicotti but think it's a bother to prepare just for yourself, try this delicious omelet.

1 egg
1 tablespoon whole wheat flour
1 tablespoon milk
salt
pepper
¼ cup ricotta cheese
¼ cup shredded mozzarella and provolone cheeses,
    combined in any proportion
pinch oregano
1 tablespoon minced parsley
pepper
oil/butter
about ½ tablespoon grated Parmesan cheese
¼ cup tomato sauce (optional)

Beat together egg, flour, and milk. Season lightly with salt and pepper. Combine ricotta, mozzarella and provolone, oregano, parsley, and a generous amount of pepper.

Heat enough oil and/or butter to cover a 6- to 8-inch omelet pan. (A well-seasoned pan will only need about ¼ tablespoon fat.) When hot, pour in the egg and cook, lifting as edges set to let unset egg run underneath. When top is soft but no longer runny, loosen entire omelet so it is free of the pan.

Place the ricotta mixture on half the omelet and fold to enclose the filling. Cover the pan and let cook for 3 to 5 minutes to heat through. Sprinkle with Parmesan cheese and slide onto a plate. Serve with tomato sauce if desired.

Serves 1

Major Protein

Note: To serve 2, double all the ingredients, but increase the number of eggs to 3. Prepare in a 10- to 12-inch skillet and cut in half to serve.

ONE-POT BAKED MACARONI AND CHEESE

2¼ cups uncooked whole grain elbows, spirals,
   or small shells
1 cup shredded cheddar or cheese of choice
1½ cups milk
2 tablespoons whole grain cracker or dried bread
   crumbs
1 tablespoon wheat germ
½ tablespoon butter

Preheat oven to 350°F. Combine pasta and shredded cheese in a greased, shallow 1-quart casserole. Add milk. Cover and bake for 30 minutes. Mix halfway through to submerge pasta in milk.

After 30 minutes, remove cover from casserole. Combine crumbs and wheat germ and sprinkle mixture over casserole; dot the top with butter and return to oven uncovered for 10 minutes.

Serves 2

Major Protein

Note: Since most natural cheeses are not colored, this dish will be creamy white rather than yellow.

STOVE-TOP MACARONI AND CHEESE

If you are willing to dirty two pots, this is very quick and extremely tasty.

3 to 4 cups uncooked whole grain spirals, elbows,
   or small shells (or 4 to 6 cups cooked)
1 tablespoon butter
2 cups shredded cheddar cheese mixed with a little
   Gouda, Edam, or Jack
⅓ cup milk
¼ teaspoon prepared mustard
1½ teaspoons soy sauce
⅛ teaspoon cayenne

Cook pasta in boiling salted water until tender, about 12 minutes, and drain.

Meanwhile, melt butter in a small saucepan; add cheese and stir with a wire whisk over low heat until it begins to melt. Add the milk and seasoning and continue to cook and stir until smooth.

Add the pasta to the sauce, mix well, and serve.

Serves 4

Major Protein

Variations: For *Superb Macaroni and Cheese,* turn into a shallow baking dish and place in a 350°F. oven for about 10 minutes. For *Sensational Macaroni and Cheese,* top the casserole with bread crumbs and dot with butter before baking.

ITALIAN MACARONI AND CHEESE

1 quart undrained canned tomatoes
2 cups uncooked small pasta
1 tablespoon nutritional yeast
½ cup shredded provolone cheese
1 cup shredded mozzarella cheese
1 teaspoon crushed oregano
½ teaspoon dried basil
¼ cup yogurt
2 tablespoons grated Parmesan cheese

Preheat oven to 350°F.

Bring tomatoes to a boil, add pasta, and cook for 10 to 12 minutes until pasta is al dente. Stir in yeast to thicken. Remove from heat and add cheese and seasonings.

Pour into 1-quart casserole, top with yogurt and grated cheese, and bake for about 10 minutes until bubbly.

Serves 2 generously or 3 modestly.

Major Protein

Variation: For a one-pot, fast-food meal just stir cheese and seasonings into pasta and tomatoes over low heat to melt. Remove from heat and add yogurt.

TOMATO SHELLS

Homemade "canned" spaghetti.

¼ cup oil
3 cups uncooked small whole grain shells or elbows
¼ cup chopped onion
½ cup chopped celery
½ cup chopped green pepper
1 clove garlic, minced
4 cups tomato juice
½ teaspoon salt
¼ teaspoon hot pepper sauce

Heat oil in a 3-quart saucepan and sauté pasta, vegetables, and garlic over moderate heat for about 10 minutes until pasta begins to color slightly. Stir occasionally. Add tomato juice and seasonings; bring to a boil. Cover and simmer over low heat for about 20 minutes until pasta is tender.

Serves 4
Protein Complement
Menu Suggestion: Complete with a generous amount of grated cheese or include beans or cheese on the menu.

ITALIAN SPAGHETTI STEW

A rich stew that includes chunks of corn on the cob for a taste and textural change; eating with fingers is definitely permitted.

1 tablespoon oil
1 large clove garlic, chopped
2 quarts canned, undrained tomatoes
1 teaspoon dried basil
1 teaspoon crushed oregano
½ pound whole grain spaghetti
2 cups cooked chick-peas
4 ears corn on the cob, cut into 2-inch segments
2 cups shredded romaine or other leafy greens
grated Parmesan cheese

Heat oil in a 3- to 5-quart pot and sauté garlic briefly. Before it begins to color, add tomato and seasonings; bring to a boil and simmer for 10 minutes.

Add the spaghetti, chick-peas, and corn, and simmer for 15 to 20 minutes, or until spaghetti is tender. Add the greens and cook 2 minutes longer, just to wilt.

Taste for seasoning, adding salt if necessary. Serve with a generous amount of Parmesan cheese.

Serves 4 to 6
Major Protein

ZITI WITH CHEESE

½ pound whole grain ziti or spirals
1½ cups diced mozzarella and provolone cheese,
    combined in any proportion
¼ cup grated Parmesan cheese
½ cup minced parsley
1 teaspoon dried basil
2 cloves garlic, split
2 tablespoons oil (at least part olive preferred)
pepper

Bring a pot of water to a boil, salt lightly, and cook pasta
until just tender, about 12 minutes. Combine cheeses,
parsley, and basil.

Put split cloves of garlic in a small saucepan or heatproof
measuring cup with oil and cook slowly over low heat until
garlic is just brown. Discard garlic.

Drain pasta. Return to the pot and toss with cheeses,
herbs, and hot garlic oil. Warm gently until cheese softens
but still holds its shape. Season liberally with pepper.

Serves 4
Major Protein

BAKED ZITI

½ pound whole grain ziti, spirals, or small shells
    (or 4 to 5 cups cooked)
2 cups tomato sauce
1 cup ricotta cheese
4 ounces thinly sliced mozzarella cheese or a
    combination of mozzarella and provolone cheeses

Preheat oven to 350°F. Cook pasta in boiling salted
water until barely tender, about 10 minutes. Drain.

Combine pasta, tomato sauce, and ricotta in a 2-quart baking dish. Top with cheese slices. Bake for about 15 minutes until very hot and cheese is melted.

Serves 4

Major Protein

CREAMY PASTA WITH CHEESE

This rich Parmesan cheese sauce is reminiscent of Fettuccine Alfredo with less fat and far fewer calories.

½ pound whole grain or spinach linguini
2 tablespoons butter
1 cup ricotta cheese
½ cup yogurt
1 cup grated Parmesan cheese
pepper

Bring a pot of water to a boil, salt lightly, and cook pasta for 10 to 12 minutes, or until cooked to taste. Drain. Return pasta to the pot, add butter, and toss over low heat until butter melts and coats pasta. If pasta seems a bit dry, add a little oil to coat completely.

Stir ricotta and yogurt into pasta and gradually add Parmesan cheese, stirring continuously until sauce is warm and creamy and cheese melts. Season liberally with pepper and serve.

Serves 4

Major Protein

Note: The success of this dish depends on using freshly grated cheese of good quality. Parmesan, romano, locatelli, pecorino, or a similar hard grating cheese can be used.

Variation: For *Creamy Pasta with Cheese and Herbs* add ⅓ cup chopped scallion, ⅓ cup minced parsley, and 2 tablespoons minced fresh basil with the butter, and proceed as above.

SPAGHETTI FANTASY

Spaghetti studded with herbs, nuts, and olives

   ½ pound whole grain spaghetti
   3 tablespoons oil (at least part olive)
   2 to 3 cloves garlic, chopped
   1 cup sliced almonds, peanuts, or sunflower seeds
      (preferably a combination)
   ½ cup chopped olives
   ½ cup chopped sweet red or green pepper
   ½ cup minced parsley
   2 tablespoons minced fresh basil or 1 teaspoon
      dried
   grated Parmesan cheese

Cook the pasta in boiling salted water until tender, about 12 minutes.

Drain the spaghetti and combine the oil and garlic in the spaghetti cooking pot. Cook about 1 minute, or until garlic just begins to color.

Add spaghetti, nuts, olives, sweet pepper, and herbs to the garlic oil and heat through, mixing until the pasta is well coated. Serve, adding cheese to taste at the table.

Serves 4

Minor Protein

Menu Suggestions: This crunchy pasta dish could use a slight protein boost, although if served with a generous amount of grated cheese on top, it can stand alone. Otherwise, a cheese- or bean-based appetizer or protein-rich salad is suggested.

PEANUT BUTTER PASTA

Pasta with a light peanut flavor.

½ pound whole grain spaghetti
½ cup chopped onion
½ cup slivered green pepper
1 tablespoon oil
½ cup warm water
4 tablespoons peanut butter
2 tomatoes, diced
1½ cups tomato juice
½ teaspoon oregano
coarsely chopped peanuts

Cook the spaghetti in boiling salted water for 10 to 12 minutes to taste. Drain.

While the spaghetti cooks, sauté the onion and pepper in oil for about 5 minutes until wilted. Stir water gradually into peanut butter until smooth and add with tomatoes, tomato juice, and oregano to onion and pepper mixture. Bring to a boil, stirring occasionally to make a smooth sauce.

Spoon hot sauce over pasta and top with chopped peanuts.

Serves 4
Minor Protein

HUNGARIAN CABBAGE NOODLES

A platter of noodles topped with cottage cheese and caraway-flavored cabbage.

   2 tablespoons butter, oil, or a combination
   1½ pounds cabbage, cut into thin strips (about 10 cups)
   2 tablespoons caraway seeds
   1 pound whole wheat noodles
   3 cups (1½ pounds) cottage cheese at room temperature

Heat butter or oil in a large skillet or wok, add the cabbage, and stir to coat well. Sprinkle with caraway, cover, and cook about 10 minutes; cabbage should still be a little crisp when done rather than soft or soggy.

While cabbage cooks, cook noodles until tender. Drain noodles, place on a serving platter, top with cottage cheese, and cover with cabbage.

Serves 6

Major Protein

Menu Suggestions: A fresh fruit appetizer, a salad featuring tomatoes, carrots, or beets, plus pickles and a dense whole grain bread will round out the menu.

STEAMED VEGETABLES WITH CHEESE

A platter of steamed vegetables topped with a rich cheese sauce can be a substantial main dish.

1 pound vegetables (individually or in combination):
  broccoli
  cauliflower
  green beans
  potatoes
¾ cup Double Cheese Sauce (page 173)

Prepare vegetables (dividing broccoli into trees and peeling the outer layer of stems if tough, dividing cauliflower into large buds, trimming ends of beans, and cutting unpeeled potatoes into halves or quarters).

Place vegetables in a steamer. If cooking more than one vegetable, add in stages to allow for varying cooking times. (Potatoes will need about 20 minutes, broccoli 12 to 15 minutes, green beans 10 minutes, and cauliflower 8 to 10 minutes, so they should be cooked in this order.) Steam until fork-tender.

Prepare sauce while vegetables steam. Place hot vegetables on serving plates and smother with sauce.

Serves 2
Major Protein

AIOLI WITH VEGETABLES

This dish, which originated in the south of France, is a simple platter of cooked vegetables and beans topped with aioli, a garlic-laden sauce. We have refined the traditional Provençal recipe to provide a less fatty, more nourishing main dish. This is easy to prepare for any number of people.

    ¾ cup yogurt
    ¼ cup mayonnaise
    1 clove garlic, minced
    ½ pound potatoes
    about 1 pound assorted vegetables: carrots,
        cauliflower, broccoli, leeks, parsnips, zucchini,
        green beans, bean sprouts, etc.
    1 onion, cut into crescents
    1 cup cooked beans, drained

Prepare sauce by mixing yogurt, mayonnaise, and garlic; allow this sauce to develop flavor at room temperature while vegetables cook.

Cut potatoes into quarters and begin steaming. They will take about 20 minutes to become tender. Meanwhile, cut other vegetables into 1-inch chunks and add to steamer at appropriate intervals so that they will all be done at the same time. (Allow 12 to 15 minutes for broccoli, carrots, and leeks, 10 minutes for parsnips and green beans, 8 to 10 minutes for cauliflower, zucchini, and bean sprouts.) During the last 10 minutes, place onion over the other vegetables. Heat beans in a separate pot.

Arrange vegetables and beans on a serving platter or spoon some of each onto individual plates. Top with generous amounts of sauce.

Serves 2
Major Protein

VEGETABLES WITH CURRY CREAM

This platter of cooked vegetables in a flavorful protein-rich sauce may be served either warm or cold.

about 1 pound assorted steamed vegetables
1 cup cooked beans, drained
1 stalk celery, chopped
2 scallions, thinly sliced
¾ cup yogurt
¼ cup mayonnaise
1 tablespoon curry powder
1 tablespoon lemon juice

Arrange vegetables with beans and celery on a serving platter in individual piles or combined. Serve scallions in a separate bowl. Mix remaining ingredients for sauce, which should also be served separately. To serve, let everyone help themselves to some of the vegetables, adding sauce and scallions as they wish.

Serves 2

Major Protein

Note: For a *Curried Vegetable Sandwich*, stuff some cooked vegetables and beans into pockets of pita bread. Top each half with ¼ cup of sauce plus some raw celery and scallion.

Menu Suggestions: If beans are not among the vegetables chosen, serve with a lentil dish. Accompany entrée with pita bread or chapatis, or serve on a base of cooked grain.

MAIN DISH STIR-FRY

Wok-cooked tofu and vegetables combine to make an Oriental short order meal. Use carrots, broccoli, cauliflower, green pepper, zucchini, Chinese greens, celery, bean sprouts, asparagus, snow peas, green beans, mushrooms, or any other vegetable you wish. Serve over brown rice or crumbled rice crackers.

    2 tablespoons oil
    1 clove garlic, cut in half
    4 scallions, cut into 1-inch sections
    1 pound fresh or frozen tofu or tempeh, cut into
      strips
    8 cups mixed vegetables in any proportion, cut
      attractively into bite-size pieces
    ½ cup water
    2 tablespoons soy sauce
    2 tablespoons cooking sherry or vinegar
    2 teaspoons sesame oil or hot oil

Heat oil in a wok and stir-fry garlic, scallions, and tofu or tempeh over medium high heat until lightly colored. Add vegetables and stir-fry 5 to 8 minutes longer until vegetables are crisp-tender. Add water, soy sauce, and sherry or vinegar; cover and cook over low heat for 5 minutes. Stir in oil and serve at once.

Serves 4

Major Protein served over grain

Note: For additional seasoning at the table, offer Chinese mustard and soy sauce.

VEGETABLES MOZZARELLA

The vegetable can be varied with the season, choosing from broccoli, zucchini, eggplant, or even green beans or asparagus.

1 tablespoon oil
1 clove garlic, minced
2 cups chopped fresh tomato or 1½ cups lightly drained canned tomato pulp
½ tablespoon chopped fresh basil or ½ teaspoon dried
½ teaspoon oregano
¼ teaspoon salt
dash honey (optional)
¾ pound vegetable of choice, cut into individual spears or half-inch rounds, depending on your selection
1 tablespoon nutritional yeast or ½ tablespoon tomato paste (optional)
3 ounces sliced or shredded mozzarella cheese (about ¾ cup)

Heat oil in a skillet and sauté garlic until it just begins to color. Add tomatoes and seasonings and simmer until soft and slightly reduced, about 10 minutes. If tomatoes are very acid, add honey.

Place vegetables in sauce, cover and simmer until just fork-tender, 15 to 20 minutes.

Remove cover and, if sauce is watery, stir in yeast or tomato paste to thicken. Top with cheese, cover and cook briefly to melt.

Serves 2

Minor Protein

Menu Suggestions: There will be adequate protein at this meal if you serve the vegetables on a bed of pasta or, if you like, polenta. A marinated bean salad provides an excellent contrast in flavor and texture.

SKILLET STEW

Fresh vegetables under a blanket of cheese.

1 tablespoon oil
1 small onion, chopped
1 small clove garlic, chopped
¼ cup chopped green pepper
3 cups sliced summer squash (about ¾ pound)
1 tomato, diced
salt
pepper
1 cup shredded cheddar cheese

Heat oil in a 10- to 12-inch skillet and sauté onion, garlic, and green pepper for 3 minutes. Add squash and tomato; cover and cook over low heat for 10 to 15 minutes until tender. Season vegetables lightly with salt and pepper. Cover with cheese. Remove from heat, cover, and let stand for 5 minutes to melt.

Serves 2

Major Protein

Variations: Substitute green beans, broccoli, or corn for squash, or use a combination of vegetables.

Menu Suggestions: Can be served on a grain or pasta, or accompanied by a muffin (see Quick Mixes). Complete the meal with a tossed salad.

SKILLET CORN, CHILIES AND CHEESE

A quick and easy vegetable entrée to serve on rice or crisp tacos.

1 tablespoon oil
1 clove garlic, chopped
1 small onion, chopped
4-ounce can chilies, drained
2 cups fresh corn kernels
½ teaspoon salt
4 ounces mild cheddar, Jack, or mozzarella cheese,
    cut in cubes
yogurt

Heat oil in a skillet and sauté garlic and onion until soft but not brown, about 3 minutes. Cut chilies into 1-inch strips and add to pan along with corn and salt. Cover and cook over low heat until corn is tender. This will take from 5 to 10 minutes, depending on the age of the corn.

Add cheese cubes, cover, and cook without stirring until cheese runs. Be sure to wait until just before serving to add the cheese, as it toughens on reheating. Serve on a base of your choice (rice, tacos, or even toast) and top with spoonfuls of yogurt.

Serves 2

Major Protein

Note: Although this is best when made with fresh corn, frozen corn can be used. For reduced calories, spoon the mixture over crisp lettuce leaves.

Variations: Substitute cooked kidney, pinto, lima, or soybeans for one third of the corn.

RYEBURGERS

Bread is the basis of this burger and it is more tasty than the ingredients might lead you to believe. Two ryeburgers and a salad make a very nice meal.

catsup
1 slice thin whole grain rye bread
relish
sliced onion (optional)
1½ to 2 ounces sliced cheese
butter/oil

Spread a thin layer of catsup on bread, top with relish and onion, if desired, and cover completely with cheese. Heat enough butter alone or with oil to cover the surface of a skillet. Add bread and cook until bottom browns. Cover pan and cook over low heat about a minute until cheese melts.

Makes 1 burger
Major Protein

RICOTTA-STUFFED PEPPERS

Cooked entirely on top of the stove.

4 medium green peppers
2 cups ricotta cheese
1 cup shredded mozzarella cheese
2 tablespoons grated Parmesan cheese
1 egg
½ teaspoon oregano
2 cups Italian-style tomato sauce well flavored with garlic, basil, and oregano

Cut peppers in half through the stem. Remove seeds and any thick inside ribs.

Mix cheeses with egg and oregano. Stuff into pepper halves.

Heat sauce in a skillet large enough to hold peppers in a single layer. When simmering, arrange peppers, stuffing side up, in sauce; cover and simmer over low heat for about 20 minutes until pepper is tender, but still crisp. Spoon sauce on top to serve.

Serves 4
Major Protein

GERMAN-STYLE NEW POTATOES

Potatoes mixed with seasoned cottage cheese; a relative of noodles and cheese.

  2 pounds (16 to 24) new or small potatoes
  2 cups cottage cheese
  4 chopped scallions
  1 tablespoon caraway seeds
  yogurt
  salt
  pepper

Steam whole unpeeled potatoes until fork-tender, about 30 minutes. Meanwhile, combine cottage cheese, scallions, and caraway seeds in a serving bowl and let stand at room temperature. Add hot, cooked potatoes, leaving them whole or cut in halves. Mix and serve at once, letting each person add yogurt individually at the table, as well as salt and pepper to taste.

Serves 4
Major Protein

FLUFFY STUFFED BAKED POTATOES

A simple baked potato can become a substantial main dish when its insides are scooped out, whipped and seasoned, and stuffed back into the skin. This should be especially good news to those who routinely pass up potatoes in favor of what they believe to be more nutritious, less fattening dishes on the menu. The fact is, in each of the following variations you get main-dish quality protein with fewer than 300 calories.

4 baked potatoes, freshly made or prepared in
   advance (see page 134)
½ teaspoon salt
pepper
½ cup yogurt
¼ cup nonfat dry milk powder
1 egg, lightly beaten (desirable but optional)
1 cup cottage cheese
¼ cup minced scallions
2 tablespoons minced green pepper

Preheat oven to 350° to 375°F.

If potato is hot, hold it in a kitchen towel. Cut in half lengthwise and let the steam escape. Holding the potato halves in a towel, carefully scoop out the pulp, leaving the shell intact.

Mash potato thoroughly by hand, wire whip, rotary or electric beater, or by pureeing in a food mill. If using a food processor, be very cautious not to over-process, turning the potatoes into a soft, gluey paste.

Beat remaining ingredients into potato puree and mound back into shells.

Return to the oven and bake for 15 to 20 minutes until hot and lightly crusted on top.

Makes 8 halves; serves 4 as an entrée, 8 as an accompaniment.

Major Protein

Note: If the idea of a potato as the focal point of the meal does not appeal to you, you can use half the baked stuffed potato as a Minor Protein. If you like the idea but can't justify keeping the oven hot for the time it takes to bake the potatoes initially, steam them instead, then mash and season as for stuffing. Turn the recipe into *Potato Mountains* by shaping the mixture into mounds on an oiled baking sheet; dot sparingly with butter, generously with paprika, and bake as for the stuffed version.

Fluffy Stuffed Baked Potatoes can be frozen for future use. Wrap in heavy-duty foil for freezing. To use, place still wrapped and frozen in a 400 F. oven and bake for about 40 minutes until softened. Remove foil and bake for 5 to 10 minutes longer until hot and crusty.

Variations: For *Creamy Stuffed Baked Potatoes,* fold 1½ cups diced melting cheese like mozzarella, provolone, Swiss, or Jack into mashed potato mixture. Mound back into skins and sprinkle liberally with paprika. Bake as above.

For *Stuffed Blue Cheese Potatoes,* reduce salt to ¼ teaspoon and cottage cheese to ½ cup. Omit scallion and green pepper. Add ½ cup crumbled blue cheese. Mound back into skins, sprinkle with paprika, and bake as directed.

Menu Suggestions: For main dish service, accompany with salad, another cooked vegetable, and bread.

CHILI

A bowl of chili garnished at the table is as satisfying and nourishing as the most expensive restaurant meal.

2 tablespoons oil
2 cloves garlic, chopped
2 large onions, chopped
¼ teaspoon cayenne
2 tablespoons chili powder
1 teaspoon cumin
1 teaspoon oregano
1 medium green pepper, chopped
2 cups tomatoes, either drained canned or fresh chopped
4 cups cooked kidney or pinto beans, drained
1 teaspoon salt (less if beans are presalted)
1 tablespoon nutritional yeast (optional)

Heat oil in a 3-quart pot and sauté garlic for 1 minute until it begins to color. Add onion and cook for 3 minutes until softened. Add seasonings and green pepper and cook for 1 minute longer.

Add remaining ingredients, adjusting salt as needed. Bring to a boil, cover, and simmer over low heat for 20 to 30 minutes until thickened. For a hearty taste, we recommend stirring in nutritional yeast just before serving; this will add good flavor and thicken the chili slightly.

Serves 4 generously (6 if served in taco shells rather than bowls)

Protein Complement (Major Protein when served as directed in Menu Suggestions below)

Note: This recipe produces a hot but not fiery chili; increase or decrease cayenne according to your own taste.

Menu Suggestions: To make the most of the beans, serve them with chopped raw onion, shredded greens doused with fresh lemon juice, shredded cheddar cheese, or pumpkin seeds toasted in a skillet and lightly crushed, and one or more of the following:

crisp corn tacos, 2 per person
brown rice, ½ cup per person
corn bread or muffins
crushed whole wheat crackers

If you are considering another item on the menu, add an avocado salad.

SLOPPY BEANS

This quick, nourishing, hot open-face sandwich is a creamy vegetable version of Sloppy Joes.

1 tablespoon oil
¼ cup chopped onion
¼ cup chopped green pepper
2 cups cooked black, brown, or red beans, drained
2 tablespoons catsup
½ teaspoon prepared mustard
¾ cup creamed cottage cheese
¼ cup sour cream
2 to 3 whole wheat hamburger rolls or biscuits, or
  6 slices whole grain toast

Heat oil in a large skillet and sauté onion and pepper for 5 to 10 minutes until browned. Add beans and cook, mashing gently, for 2 to 3 minutes. Add remaining ingredients and stir over low heat for 5 to 10 minutes. (Depending on cottage cheese, sauce will turn completely smooth or some curds will remain.) Serve hot over bread base.
Serves 2 to 3
Major Protein

B.O.B.
(BEANS ON BOARD)

Beans in a barbecue-style sauce served on toast.

1 small onion, chopped
1 small clove garlic, chopped
1 scant tablespoon oil
1 teaspoon chili powder
1½ cups cooked kidney or pinto beans, lightly
   drained
2 tablespoons catsup
½ teaspoon molasses
dash soy sauce
tomato juice (optional)
2 tablespoons wheat germ
4 slices whole grain toast
shredded cheddar cheese

Sauté onion and garlic in oil for about 5 minutes until
they begin to color. Add chili powder and cook for 30
seconds. Stir in beans, catsup, molasses, and a little soy. If
dry, add enough tomato juice to moisten. Heat through.

Stir in wheat germ to make thick (if too dry add more
tomato juice). When hot, spoon over toast and top with
cheese.

Serves 2
Major Protein

SPINACH AND CHICK-PEAS WITH FETA

If precooked chick-peas are on hand, this dish is quick and easy as well as delicious.

3 cups cooked chick-peas, drained
½ cup bean liquid
1 tablespoon oil (olive preferred)
1 pound spinach, chopped (about 10 cups)
1 teaspoon cumin
1 tablespoon lemon juice
8 ounces (about 1⅓ cups) crumbled feta cheese
pepper

Combine beans, bean liquid, oil, spinach, and cumin in a large pot, cover and cook over low heat until spinach is tender and everything else is quite hot. This will take 5 to 10 minutes.

Stir in lemon juice, crumble in feta, add a generous amount of pepper, and remove from heat. Serve hot or at room temperature.

Serves 6
Major Protein

BEAN BURGERS

Cooked indoors or out these can be served as you would any other burger on a bun with a choice of "fixings." Top with cheese for a cheeseburger.

1⅓ cups sunflower seeds, or 2 cups sunflower meal
   (ground sunflower seeds)
4 cups cooked red or pink beans, drained
½ cup chopped onion
1 teaspoon chili powder
about 1 teaspoon salt (omit with well-salted beans)
3 to 4 tablespoons catsup
wheat germ

Using a processor fitted with a steel cutting blade grind seeds to a fine meal (or use preground meal) and transfer to a large mixing bowl. Grind beans.

Mix ground beans, onion, chili powder, and salt to taste with the seed meal. Add sufficient catsup to make the mixture damp enough to mold, without being soft. If too soft, add wheat germ as needed.

Shape into patties, using about ⅓ cup for each.

To cook, sauté in oil, or bake in a 350°F. oven about 20 minutes until brown and crusty on the surface, or broil 3 inches from the heat, about 5 to 8 minutes on each side, or cook over coals until charred on each side. Cooking time on the grill will vary with the heat of the coals and the distance of the grate; since the inside is already completely cooked, you can gauge doneness by the color on the surface.

Makes 12 burgers; serves 6

Major Protein

Note: For a juicier, crustier burger, baste the surface with a little oil during baking or broiling.

SOYBURGERS

A tender, juicy burger.

1⅓ cups sunflower seeds or a combination of seeds
    and peanuts
4 cups cooked soybeans, drained
1 large onion, chopped
3 tablespoons soy sauce
wheat germ or dry whole grain bread or cracker
    crumbs

Grind seeds and nuts to a fine meal. Grind beans to a
dry pulp.

Combine ground mixtures, onion, and soy sauce. If mixture is too soft to hold shape, add some wheat germ or
crumbs. Form into patties, using ½ cup mixture for each.

To cook, bake in a 350°F. oven for 20 minutes, or broil
about 3 inches from heat for 5 to 8 minutes per side until
browned, or cook on a grill over coals.

Makes 8 burgers; serves 4

Major Protein

Variation: For *Onion Soyburgers*, sauté a little chopped
onion and garlic in some oil, then add patties and pan-fry.

BOSTON ROAST

This American bean roast was popularized in the meat-saving era of World War II. It is tender and flavorful, good plain or with tomato sauce, and the cold leftovers can be used for sandwiches.

1 cup soft whole wheat bread crumbs or 2 slices
  whole grain bread
1½ cups grated cheese
2 cups cooked kidney beans or other red beans,
  drained and ground or chopped fine
¼ cup wheat germ
1 teaspoon grated onion
1 teaspoon to 1 tablespoon chili powder (depending
  on personal preference)
1 teaspoon salt (omit if beans are salted)
pepper

Preheat oven to 350°F. Prepare bread crumbs, grated cheese, and ground beans (in that order if using the same utensil to avoid washing). Combine all ingredients and shape into a single loaf or 4 individual mounds on an oiled baking sheet. Bake for about 30 minutes until crusty, basting once or twice with oil during cooking.

Serves 4
Major Protein

PEANUT BUTTER LOAF

One of the easiest nut-grain loaves to assemble and very good eating served plain or with catsup or mustard.

1 cup peanut butter
1 cup soft whole wheat bread crumbs
1 cup cooked brown rice
1 stalk celery, chopped
1 egg, beaten
1 cup milk
1 teaspoon soy sauce

Preheat oven to 350°F. Combine all ingredients in a mixing bowl and stir until evenly blended. Place in a well-oiled 8-inch loaf pan and bake for 45 minutes until top is firm and brown. Cool for at least 10 minutes in pan before turning out. Serve warm, at room temperature, or chilled.

Serves 4 to 6

Major Protein

Menu Suggestions: Serve with any fresh vegetables and a fruit or vegetable salad. For a more substantial meal, begin with a light vegetable soup.

LAYERED TOMATO CASSEROLE

1 pound tomatoes (3 medium)
1 cup fresh whole wheat bread crumbs
¼ cup wheat germ
1 cup grated cheese
½ teaspoon salt
¼ cup chopped onion
2 tablespoons minced parsley
1 teaspoon dried basil
2 tablespoons butter

Preheat oven to 350°F. Slice tomatoes thin. Combine bread crumbs, wheat germ, cheese, and salt.

Butter a shallow 1-quart baking dish and layer one third crumb mixture, one half tomato slices, one half chopped onion, 1 tablespoon parsley, and ½ teaspoon basil. Repeat the layers and top with remaining crumb mixture. Dot with butter. Bake for about 30 minutes until browned.

Serves 2 to 3

Major Protein

Note: To serve 4 to 6, double the recipe and bake in a shallow 9 × 13-inch pan.

MATZO LASAGNE

Elements from two different worlds form a happy liaison that is easy to make using basic pantry ingredients.

2 medium onions, thinly sliced
6 whole wheat matzos
3 cups cottage cheese
1 cup shredded mozzarella cheese
½ cup shredded cheddar cheese
4 medium tomatoes, sliced, or 2 cups canned,
   drained tomatoes
½ teaspoon salt
pepper
1½ cups tomato juice

Preheat oven to 350°F. Place half the onion slices in a shallow 2-quart baking dish generously greased with oil. Cover with 2 of the matzos, broken into pieces if necessary. Top with half the cottage cheese, half the mozzarella, half the cheddar, and half the tomatoes. Season with half the salt and pepper. Top with 2 more matzos, remaining onion, cottage cheese, mozzarella, cheddar, tomato, and seasonings. Cover with last 2 matzos. Pour juice evenly over top; cover and bake for 20 minutes.

Uncover, sprinkle with additional cheese if desired, and bake 10 minutes longer. Let sit at room temperature for 10 minutes before serving.

Serves 4 to 6
Major Protein
Note: Transfer any leftovers to a pan that holds them comfortably and refrigerate. To restore, add a little tomato juice, cover and bake in a 350° to 375°F. oven for about 10 minutes until hot and bubbly. Uncover, top with some shredded cheese, and return to the oven to melt.

BISCUIT-CRUST PIZZA

A very good spur-of-the-moment pizza can be made by using biscuit dough rather than a yeast-leavened crust. This makes a thicker, cakier base, more like the Sicilian-style pie.

Biscuit Crust

2¼ cups whole wheat flour
¼ cup wheat germ
3 teaspoons baking powder
½ teaspoon salt
¼ cup oil
1 teaspoon honey
⅔ cup water
cornmeal

Topping

2 cups drained canned or stewed tomatoes, or 1½
   cups tomato sauce
1½ cups shredded mozzarella cheese
¼ cup grated Parmesan cheese
salt
pepper
oregano
oil

Preheat oven to 425°F.

Combine the flour, wheat germ, baking powder, and salt in a large mixing bowl.

Pour in the oil and mix with a fork until it is evenly dispersed.

Add the honey and water all at once and mix dough gently and thoroughly until it holds together. If it is too crumbly, add a few more tablespoons water as needed.

Oil a jellyroll pan, 14-inch pizza pan, or baking sheet and dust with cornmeal. Moisten hands and press dough gently into pan to form a *thin* crust over the entire surface. Keep dough uniform in thickness and do not raise the crust at the edges. Bake for about 8 minutes.

Spread the tomatoes over the entire crust area. Top with the cheeses. Season lightly with salt and generously with pepper and oregano. Drizzle a little oil over all.

Return to the oven for 12 to 15 minutes.

Serves 3 to 4
Major Protein

QUICK, CREAMY ONION PIE

The richness of the filling is surprising in view of the modest ingredients. This is an extremely easy pie to make.

   1 9-inch Caraway Cracker Crumb Crust (recipe
      on page 112)
   3 large onions, thinly sliced
   1 tablespoon oil
   1 tablespoon butter
   2 cups creamed cottage cheese
   ¼ teaspoon salt
   pepper
   ⅛ teaspoon cayenne
   1 teaspoon paprika

Preheat oven to 400°F. Bake crust for about 10 minutes until lightly colored. While crust bakes, combine onions, oil and butter in a 1-quart pot. Cover and stew over low heat for 10 minutes until onion is softened.

Mix cottage cheese with salt and pepper. Place in baked crust. Top with onions and distribute cayenne and paprika evenly over surface.

Return to oven for 15 minutes. Let sit for at least 10 minutes before serving; serve while still warm or at room temperature. Chill leftovers and serve cold.

Serves 4
Major Protein
Menu Suggestions: Serve with a large salad or a cooked vegetable plate.

CARAWAY CRACKER CRUMB CRUST

¾ cup rye, corn, or whole wheat cracker crumbs
   or a combination
½ cup wheat germ
½ tablespoon caraway seeds
¼ teaspoon salt
2 tablespoons oil

Combine crumbs, wheat germ, caraway seeds, and salt.
Stir in oil until completely moistened. Press over bottom
and sides of a 9-inch pie pan. Chill for at least 15 minutes
or prebake in a 400°F. oven, depending on recipe directions.
Makes a 9-inch pie crust

TOFU WITH ONIONS AND CHEESE

Adapted from the wonderful *Book of Tofu*, this recipe for stewed onions with a tofu and cheese topping affords a good introduction to tofu.

2 tablespoons oil
4 medium to large onions, thinly sliced
¼ cup soy sauce
1 pound tofu
1 tablespoon sherry
4 ounces Muenster cheese, thinly sliced or shredded
  (about 1 cup)

Combine oil, onions, and 2 tablespoons soy sauce in a 15-inch skillet. Cover and cook over low heat for 10 minutes until softened.

While onions cook, slice tofu ¼ inch thick and press it to expel moisture. (See page 239.) When onions have softened, remove tofu from pressing cloth and cut into cubes.

Add remaining soy sauce, sherry, and tofu to onions; cover and cook for 10 minutes. Top with cheese, remove pan from heat, cover and let stand for a few minutes until cheese melts.

Serves 4

Major Protein

Menu Suggestions: Serve on rice, rice crackers, or toast if desired, with a vegetable and salad on the side.

TOFU À LA KING

Here's a new slant on the old-fashioned à la king sauce and it's hard to notice the change. Serve in the customary way on biscuits or on a base of toast or whole grain muffins.

¾ pound frozen tofu
1 cup cold water
2 tablespoons soy sauce
2 tablespoons butter
1 medium onion, chopped
¼ cup chopped green pepper
2 cups diced mushrooms
¼ cup whole wheat flour
1½ cups milk
½ cup chopped pimiento
3 tablespoons sherry
½ teaspoon salt
dash hot pepper sauce
2 small biscuits, 2 slices unbuttered toast, or 1 large
    muffin per serving.

Unwrap tofu and place in a bowl. Cover with boiling water and let stand while preparing remaining ingredients. When defrosted, drain and squeeze each piece dry between your palms. Combine cold water and soy sauce and marinate tofu while cooking sauce.

Melt butter in a 1- to 1½-quart saucepan. Sauté onion, green pepper, and mushrooms for about 5 minutes, until soft and moist. Stir in flour, then gradually add milk.

Cook over medium heat, stirring frequently, until thick and bubbling, about 5 minutes.

Drain tofu and press once again between palms to expel moisture. Tear into bite-size pieces.

Add tofu, pimiento, and seasonings to sauce and cook, stirring, for about 5 minutes to heat through. Adjust seasonings to taste.

Spoon over bread base to serve.

Serves 4

Major Protein

Variation: For a more colorful sauce, ½ cup frozen peas can be added with the tofu.

Menu Suggestions: A green salad is a must, and cooked carrots are a good accompaniment if you want another vegetable.

ARROZ CON QUESO

This version of rice, chilies, and cheese is based on pre-cooked rice and is prepared in the oven.

4 cups cooked brown rice
½ teaspoon salt (if rice is unseasoned)
½ cup chopped scallions
**1 4-ounce can whole green chilies, drained and cut
    into wide strips**
1 cup farmer or dry curd (pot style) cottage cheese
**1½ cups shredded or 6 ounces sliced Jack or
    Muenster cheese**
½ cup shredded cheddar cheese

Preheat oven to 350°F.

Season rice with salt if needed; add scallions.

Place half the rice in a greased 2-quart casserole. Top with half the chilies.

If Jack or Muenster cheese has been shredded, combine it with the cottage cheese and spread over the rice and chilies. If cheese is sliced, top rice and chilies with the cottage cheese, then layer cheese on top.

Cover with remaining rice, sprinkle with shredded cheddar, and arrange remaining chili strips over all.

Bake for 30 minutes.

Serves 4 to 6

Major Protein

Note: This dish can also be made with brown rice that has been cooked in a seasoned or light tomato broth.

BAKED RICE AND BLUE CHEESE

A casserole for blue cheese lovers made with precooked rice.

4 cups cooked brown rice
¼ cup lemon juice
1 teaspoon dry mustard
4 scallions, sliced
1 cup yogurt
½ cup sliced olives
4 ounces blue cheese, cut into small cubes (about ½ cup)

Preheat oven to 350°F.

Combine all ingredients, tossing gently so that the cheese remains in chunks.

Place in an oiled 9-inch or 1½-quart baking dish; cover and bake for 20 minutes.

Serves 4

Minor Protein

Main Dish Salads

CHEF'S SPECIAL SALAD OR SALAD BAR

This meal is dependent on the whims of the salad maker. The more you add, the better the salad will be—the list of ingredients below is just a start. Assemble the salad in the kitchen or serve the ingredients separately buffet style.

mixed greens
raw vegetables cut into bite-size pieces, including:

broccoli	scallions or red onion
cauliflower	tomato
green beans	mushrooms
cucumber	jicima
zucchini	grated raw carrots
avocado	grated raw beets
radish	sprouts

cooked beans or sliced cooked potatoes
2 tablespoons toasted pumpkin seeds per serving
1 4-ounce square tofu, diced, per serving
½ cup shredded or crumbled cheese per serving, including:

feta	Jack
blue	cheddar
cottage	Cheeson (page 42)
Swiss	

sliced hard-cooked egg
dressing of choice

Tear greens into bite-size pieces. Combine all ingredients as desired in a salad bowl. Dress to taste.

Major Protein

STUFFED AVOCADO SALAD

mixed greens
½ avocado, cut lengthwise through stem end
lemon wedge
½ cup cottage cheese
shredded carrots
shredded beets
chopped scallions
alfalfa sprouts
tomato wedges or orange sections
cooked chick-peas or toasted pumpkin seeds
olives
celery sticks
Dressing (optional): Creamy Tofu Garlic (page 163),
    Light French Tomato (page 162), or Thick Creamy
    Blue Cheese (page 163)

Cover serving plate generously with greens. Remove pit
from avocado half and sprinkle exposed surface with lemon
juice. Avocado can be left in the shell, or skin can be
removed with a sharp paring knife.

Mound cottage cheese in the cavity left by the pit and
place the stuffed avocado on the greens. Top the cottage
cheese with carrots, beets, scallions, and sprouts, letting the
excess flow over onto the greens. Surround with any of the
remaining ingredients you wish and dress to taste. (You
may not even need dressing, as the cottage cheese makes
the vegetables moist.)

Serves 1

Major Protein

Variations: For *Hot Stuffed Avocado Salad*, fill the avocado
hollow with ½ cup cottage cheese mixed with ¼ cup
shredded cheese and bake in a 375°F. oven or toaster
oven for 15 minutes.

For *Stuffed Tomato Salad*, substitute 1 medium tomato
for the avocado half, remove a slice from the top and the
meat from inside to make a hollow shell. Stuff with cottage

cheese, or prepare as for Hot Stuffed Avocado. (The inside of the tomato can be added to the other vegetables or reserved for seasoning soup, sauces, or stews.)

GREEK COUNTRY SALAD

Prepare on one large platter or divide ingredients among 4 bowls.

6 cups bite-size pieces romaine lettuce
2 tomatoes, cut in wedges
2 cups cooked chick-peas, drained
1 small cucumber, peeled and thinly sliced
1 cup (6 ounces) feta cheese, cut in small pieces
black olives
red onion, cut into thin slices
capers
pickled hot peppers (optional)
stuffed grape leaves (optional)
anchovies (optional)
salt
pepper
dried oregano
about 3 tablespoons lemon juice
about ⅓ cup olive oil

Toss lettuce with tomatoes, chick-peas, and cucumber. Top evenly with feta, olives, onion rings, and capers.

Garnish as desired with hot peppers, grape leaves, and anchovies.

Season lightly with salt (if feta is mild and anchovies excluded), and generously with pepper and oregano. Dress to taste with lemon juice and oil. Toss before serving.

Serves 4

Major Protein

Note: As an accompaniment to a meal, this will provide a Minor Protein for 6 to 8.

MEXICAN STUFFED AVOCADO SALAD

mixed greens
½ avocado, cut lengthwise through stem end
lemon wedge
½ cup cooked kidney or pinto beans, drained
chopped canned chilies
¼ cup shredded Jack or cheddar cheese
yogurt, or yogurt seasoned lightly with sour cream
tomato wedges
olives
pickled hot peppers
sweet green and red pepper wedges
Dressing: Light Mexican Tomato Dressing (page
    162) or Mexican Tomato Vinaigrette (page 161)
2 taco shells

Cover serving plate generously with greens.

Remove pit from avocado half and sprinkle exposed surface with lemon juice. Avocado can either be left in the shell and scooped out with the filling as you eat, or the skin can be removed with a small, sharp paring knife.

Place avocado half on greens and fill cavity with beans mixed to taste with canned chilies. Let any excess beans flow onto greens. Top with shredded cheese and a dollop of plain or seasoned yogurt.

Surround with the remaining ingredients as desired and dress to taste. Use the tacos to shovel the salad onto the fork, or pile the salad onto the tacos and eat out of hand.

Serves 1

Major Protein

Variation: If desired, the bean-stuffed, cheese-topped avocado can be placed in a 350°F. oven or under the broiler to melt the cheese.

ILSE'S VEGETABLES IN CREAM SAUCE

A cold and tangy sauce of yogurt, sour cream, and vegetables generously ladled over warm steamed potatoes. The perfect hot-weather entrée, for which David's mother is owed the credit.

4 medium potatoes
2 medium onions, sliced
2 cups sour cream
2 cups yogurt
½ cup vinegar or pickling juice
½ teaspoon salt (omit with pickling juice)
2 small tomatoes, cut into bite-size pieces
6 radishes, sliced
1 cucumber, peeled and cubed
1 sour pickle cut into quarter-inch cubes

Cut potatoes into quarters and steam for about 15 minutes, or until tender.

Place onion slices over potatoes in steamer initially and steam for 2 minutes. Remove and run under cold water to cool.

In a large serving bowl combine sour cream, yogurt, and vinegar or pickling juice. The amount of vinegar and/or pickling juice can be adjusted to taste.

Add salt, onion, tomatoes, radishes, cucumber, and pickle, and mix gently.

Serve at once over warm potatoes, or chill if prepared in advance.

Serves 6

Minor Protein

Menu Suggestions: Be sure to include whole grain bread to eat with any extra sauce.

MACARONI AND CHEESE SALAD

Wholesome enough to serve as an entrée at lunchtime or for a light dinner.

½ cup yogurt
¼ cup mayonnaise
4 cups cooked small whole wheat pasta (elbows, spirals, shells, or broad noodles)
¼ cup chopped scallion
¼ cup chopped green pepper
1 cup tiny cubes cheddar or colby cheese
1 cup cooked beans, corn, or raw peas

Mix yogurt and mayonnaise until smooth. Add remaining ingredients and stir to coat.
Serves 4 to 6
Minor Protein; Major Protein with large portions

COLD PASTA AND BROCCOLI

A pasta salad to serve as the main course.

4 to 5 cups cooked whole grain spirals or shells (½ pound uncooked pasta)
2 cups cooked kidney beans, drained
4 cups diced, lightly steamed broccoli (about 1 pound)
6 tablespoons oil (part olive preferred)
3 tablespoons wine vinegar
1 teaspoon soy sauce
1 split clove garlic (optional)
¾ cup grated Parmesan cheese

Prepare pasta and beans if you do not have them already on hand. Steam broccoli for 8 to 10 minutes until barely tender. Combine oil, vinegar, soy sauce, and garlic, if desired, in a large, shallow serving bowl. Add pasta, beans, and broccoli, and mix well before serving. Add cheese at the table.

Serves 6

Major Protein

Note: Refrigeration is recommended if this is made more than an hour in advance, but let stand at room temperature for at least 15 minutes to remove chill before serving.

PIZZA SALAD

An excellent booster for pasta and bean-based entrées.

4 cups shredded greens
1 medium tomato, cut into thin wedges
½ cup shredded mozzarella cheese
¼ cup shredded provolone cheese
½ green pepper cut into thin slivers
¼ cup sliced olives (optional)
¼ cup sliced mushrooms (optional)
3 tablespoons grated Parmesan cheese
½ cup Light Italian Tomato Dressing (page 162)
   or Italian Tomato Vinaigrette (page 161)

Spread greens out in individual bowls or a single shallow dish. Top with tomato. Cover with shredded cheeses. Decorate with green pepper, olives, and mushrooms. Coat with grated Parmesan. Add dressing at serving time.

Serves 2

Major Protein

Side Dishes

BAKED ASPARAGUS

Fresh asparagus is crisp and in no way resembles the canned variety. Cooking fresh asparagus in the oven retains its color, flavor, and texture, and keeps it from becoming stringy.

asparagus
butter
foil

Preheat oven to 350°F. Wash asparagus and trim the tough ends. As the cooking time varies with their size, separate asparagus if of vastly different thicknesses and place each bunch on a double layer of foil. Dot lightly with butter and wrap to enclose in a foil packet. Place in the oven for about 20 minutes. This will be long enough for medium-size asparagus to become tender yet still be crunchy. Alternately, the foil-wrapped asparagus can be cooked over hot coals. Serve hot; if serving is delayed, keep wrapped.

Allow 1½ pounds to serve 4

PAN-FRIED ASPARAGUS

When asparagus is quickly stir-fried it becomes sweet and crunchy and is as much fun to eat as candy.

1½ to 2 pounds asparagus
2 tablespoons butter/oil
salt
pepper

Trim asparagus by snapping the ends and slice into 1½-inch lengths. Heat fat in a skillet or wok and stir-fry asparagus over high heat for 5 minutes until crisp-tender. Season to taste with salt and pepper.
Serves 4

CRISP FRIED BEETS

beets
oil or butter
lemon wedge

Scrub beets. Peel only if skin is tough. Shred in a food processor or hand grater. Heat fat to just cover the surface of a skillet or wok. When hot, add shredded beets and stir-fry for 3 to 5 minutes. Beets should retain their crispness. Season lightly with lemon juice and serve hot.
1 pound beets serves 4

STEAMED BROCCOLI

All parts of the broccoli are edible, including the leaves and stems. The stems are often difficult to chew because of the tough, fibrous layer on the surface. Underneath this, however, is a tender, succulent core, which is why you should peel the stalks thinly if you haven't enjoyed them up to now.

Clean broccoli, peel if desired, and separate into trees. If stalks are thick, slit to shorten cooking time.

Place on vegetable steamer and steam for 10 minutes. If not tender, cook 5 minutes longer. Serve with fresh lemon wedges.

1 pound serves 4 to 6

BUTTER-STEAMED BRUSSELS SPROUTS

10-ounce container brussels sprouts
2 tablespoons butter
fresh parsley
2 tablespoons water
salt
pepper

Wash and quarter sprouts through core. Melt butter in a skillet, wok, or saucepan and stir-fry sprouts for 5 minutes.

Add lots of fresh parsley and water; cover and steam until tender, about 10 minutes. Surfaces will brown slightly.

Season to taste with salt and pepper.

Serves 4

COOKED COLESLAW

A Pennsylvania-Dutch selection that is especially nice in the winter in place of a cold salad.

1½ tablespoons oil
4 cups coarsely shredded cabbage
½ teaspoon salt
1 tablespoon honey
2 tablespoons cider vinegar
½ teaspoon prepared mustard
½ cup yogurt

Heat oil in a large skillet or wok. Add cabbage, stir to coat with fat, and add salt. Cover and cook for 10 minutes.

Stir in honey, vinegar, and mustard and, when well blended, cover and remove from heat.

Stir yogurt into warm cabbage just before serving.

Serves 4 to 6

PAN-FRIED CABBAGE

A universally overcooked vegetable gets proper treatment here.

2 tablespoons oil/butter
3 tablespoons sesame seeds
6 cups cabbage, sliced into strips (about ¾ pound)

Heat fat in a large skillet and toast sesame seeds lightly for 1 minute. Add cabbage, stir to coat with fat and seeds, cover, and cook over medium heat for about 10 minutes until wilted. Stir once again just before serving.

Serves 4

ORANGE-GLAZED CARROTS

Carrots glazed by a delicate, sweet sauce.

   1 tablespoon butter
   1 pound carrots, cut into disks
   ½ cup orange juice
   1 tablespoon honey

Melt butter in a 1-quart saucepan or skillet. Add carrots and stir to coat. Add orange juice, cover and simmer for 10 minutes until just tender. Stir in honey, raise heat and boil rapidly, uncovered, until liquid is reduced.
Serves 4
Variation: For *Orange-Glazed Parsnips*, replace carrots with peeled, sliced parsnips.

FRESH GINGER CARROTS

   2 tablespoons butter
   1 pound carrots, cut into matchsticks (about 3 cups)
   2 teaspoons chopped fresh ginger

Melt butter in a skillet or wok and stir-fry carrots and ginger for 5 to 8 minutes until tender but still crunchy and beginning to brown. Serve hot.
Serves 4

CARROTS WITH WALNUTS

6 medium carrots
¼ cup water
2 tablespoons soy sauce
¼ cup walnut pieces

Slice carrots into thin disks. Combine with water in a small saucepan, bring to a boil, cover, and cook until just tender, 10 minutes.

Add soy sauce and walnuts and cook, stirring, over medium-high heat until moisture evaporates.

Serves 4

Variation: For *Carrots with Sunflower Seeds*, replace walnuts with sunflower seeds.

BARBECUED CORN

About as American as you can get, particularly when it's cooked under an open sky.

Place unshucked corn on a grill 4 to 6 inches above the coals. Roast for 10 minutes, turning a few times. Shuck, using a mitt to protect your hands, and return to heat for about 5 minutes, turning until lightly browned on all sides.

For delayed service, roast for about 10 minutes as described, then move to the side of the grill. Just before serving, husk and brown.

CORN ON THE COB

Contrary to popular practice, corn needs only a few minutes to cook to perfection.

unshucked corn

Bring water to a boil in a large covered pot. Do not add salt or sugar. When water is boiling, remove husks and silky strands from corn and plunge into hot water. When boiling resumes, cook for 3 minutes, then drain and serve.

Note: If you do not wish to butter your corn, try seasoning it with soy sauce.

ITALIAN SAUTÉED CUCUMBERS

2 medium cucumbers
2 tablespoons butter or a mixture of oil and butter
1 clove garlic, chopped
1 teaspoon oregano
2 tablespoons chopped fresh basil, or 2 tablespoons chopped fresh parsley plus ½ teaspoon dried basil
2 tablespoons grated Parmesan cheese
¼ teaspoon salt

Peel cucumbers and cut in ½-inch dice.

Heat fat in a skillet. Sauté garlic for 1 minute, then add cucumber, oregano, and basil. Sauté, stirring occasionally, until softened but still crunchy, about 10 to 15 minutes.

Sprinkle with cheese, salt to taste, and serve hot.

Serves 4

Variation: Replace some or all of the cucumber with zucchini but do not peel it.

STEAMED EGGPLANT NOODLES

A low-calorie, low-carbohydrate pasta substitute.

1½ pounds eggplant

Peel eggplant and cut in lengthwise slices about ¼ inch thick. Cut each slice into sticks ¼ inch wide.

Place strips of eggplant in a vegetable steamer and steam for 15 minutes until tender but not mushy. Top with sauce of choice and serve.

Serves 4

Menu Suggestions: Eggplant noodles can be served as a side dish with tomato sauce, cheese sauce, Quick Mushroom Sauce (page 182), or any similar topping. Or, prepare as an entrée topped with ricotta cheese and sauce.

STIR-FRIED GREEN BEANS WITH GARLIC

2 tablespoons oil
1 pound green beans, broken in half
6 cloves garlic, chopped
½ teaspoon salt
1 tablespoon soy sauce

Heat oil in a wok and stir-fry beans and garlic for 5 minutes. Keep heat high to singe beans.

Add seasonings, cover wok, lower heat, and stew for 5 minutes.

Serves 4

Variation: For *Stir-Fried Broccoli with Garlic*, replace beans with broccoli, using the flowers and the stems, which have been pared and sliced into thin sticks.

STEAMED GREENS

In many parts of the world, spring is greeted by city and country folk alike who comb the fields, roadsides, and vacant lots for the first spring greens. Under the tutelage of their parents, children learn at a very young age to identify many wild edibles. If you can spot dandelion greens (before the flowers come), lambsquarter, sorrel, wild mustard, and the like, you too can take part in this spring rite. If not, you can still enjoy cooked greens by preparing this dish with romaine, spinach, kale, chard, collard greens, beet greens, mustard greens, chickory, or any other leafy greens you can get hold of, preferably in a varied mix.

1 pound greens
1 tablespoon oil
1 clove garlic, chopped
salt
pepper
lemon wedges

Clean greens well and tear or shred with a knife into small pieces. (You will have about 12 cups.)

Heat oil in a large pot and cook garlic until it begins to sizzle but does not color. Add greens, cover, and cook for 5 minutes until wilted. Stir, replace cover, and continue to cook until greens are tender, 5 to 15 minutes, depending on what you have used.

Season with salt and pepper and serve with a wedge of lemon for additional seasoning at the table.

Serves 4

MUSHROOMS IN GARLIC BUTTER

16 large to 24 medium mushrooms (8 to 10 ounces)
4 tablespoons butter
2 tablespoons oil
1 cup parsley, loosely packed
2 cloves garlic, sliced
¼ medium onion, cut up
1½ teaspoons lemon juice
¼ teaspoon salt

Preheat oven to 350° to 375°F. Remove mushroom stems and reserve for another use. Clean caps and place hollow side up in a shallow baking dish.

Melt butter and puree with remaining ingredients in blender or processor. Spoon butter puree into caps, placing any extra in pan around them.

Bake about 15 minutes until hot and bubbly. Serve hot with plenty of bread to sop up the garlic butter.

Serves 4

THE STANDARD BAKED POTATO

By now most people know that it's not the potato but what we generally put on it that has given it a "fattening" reputation. The average potato furnishes no more calories than the average orange or a slice of bread. Soft and steamy inside, brown and crunchy on the surface, the baked potato really doesn't need anything at all to improve it. In case you don't agree, try any of the suggested toppings that follow the directions for baking. If you select one of the Minor Protein toppings, the baked potato will practically serve as a complete entrée.

Before we go on to tell you the right way to bake potatoes, we'd like to suggest "a potato party" for your next group function. There is no easier way to entertain than to pack your oven full of potatoes and then serve them on a platter with a broad array of toppings. It adds up to very little work for the cook, minimal clean-up, and a good time for everyone.

medium-size potatoes (about 3 per pound)

Preheat oven to 400°F. Scrub potato clean and cut out any sprouts or eyes. Dry well with paper towels. Pierce in several places with the prongs of a fork to prevent bursting in the oven. *Do not wrap in foil.*

Place on a baking sheet or directly on the rack of the oven and bake for about 45 minutes. When done, potato will yield readily to gentle pressure with a mitted hand, or a skewer will easily pierce through to the center. Naturally, larger potatoes require longer baking, small ones less.

Note: Potatoes can actually bake in oven heats ranging from 325° to 450°F. in case you want to cook them with other foods at the same time. Adjust the timing up or down according to the temperature.

When you bake potatoes directly in hot coals, wrapping in foil is recommended, but to prevent steaming the foil should have several punctures. Before serving, unwrap them and let the skin char a few minutes.

Baked Potato Toppings

Chopped pimiento
Melted lemon butter, plain or with chives
Prepared mustard
Mushrooms marinated in oil and vinegar
Guacamole (page 23)

Minor Protein Toppings

Cottage cheese and chives or scallions
Vegetable Cottage Cheese (page 27)
Whipped Cottage Cream (page 164)
Shredded cheese
Shredded cheese and a spoonful of stewed
  tomatoes
Melted mozzarella cheese and tomato sauce (for
  Potato Pizzaiola)
Feta cheese or blue cheese mashed with yogurt and
  coarse black pepper
Poached eggs
Peanut butter
Onion Dip (page 25)

PAN-ROASTED POTATOES

Steamed, then roasted potatoes combine the best of
tastes, creating a creamy interior under a very crisp cru
you don't mind using the oven, these are a lot less wor
fix and clean up after than home fries, and, in our opir
better eating.

    1½ pounds potatoes
    2 tablespoons butter or part oil and butter

Preheat oven to 375°F.

Scrub potatoes, cut into even-sized chunks, and st
for 10 minutes until partially tender.

Coat with butter in a baking dish and bake for 30 to
minutes until well browned outside and fork-tender. 1
occasionally for even browning. Particularly large pi
may need more time.

Serves 4

DAVID'S PAN FRIES

If you want to brown potatoes on the outside and get th
tender on the inside without deep-frying or preboiling th
keep the heat low under the pan and be patient. These
exceptional with eggs.

    1 to 1½ pounds potatoes
    oil
    salt
    pepper

Scrub potatoes and slice ¼ inch thick. Heat enough
to cover the surface of a heavy skillet. Add as many po
slices as will fit without piling. If you need more room,
another pan.

Cook over low heat, shaking the pan and loosening v

a spatula every so often. Check progress by lifting with tongs or a spatula (do not pierce with a fork). Keep close watch once browning begins. When potatoes are a deep bronze, turn and cook the other side. It will brown faster than the first side. Cooking time is highly variable but plan on about 45 minutes. Season to taste with salt and pepper and serve.

Serves 4

BASIC MASHED POTATOES

The addition of yogurt to mashed potatoes lends a very special flavor.

1½ pounds potatoes
½ teaspoon salt
⅛ teaspoon pepper
½ cup yogurt
¼ cup nonfat dry milk powder

Cut potatoes into quarters and steam for 15 to 20 minutes until tender. (You may peel them or not after cooking, depending on personal preference.)

Puree potatoes in a food mill, in a food processor using the plastic blade, in the blender, or whip by hand using a potato masher, beater or wire whisk.

Beat in remaining ingredients until light and fluffy.

Makes about 3 cups; 4 to 6 servings
Minor Protein

Note: For calorie counters, ½ cup mashed potatoes from this recipe furnishes only 85 calories (and 4 grams protein). If butter is essential to your enjoyment of mashed potatoes, top with melted butter to taste.

Variation: For *Surprise Mashed Potatoes*, nourishing enough to provide Major Protein as a main course, stir a little crushed garlic and 4 ounces (1 cup) diced cheese into the fresh, hot, mashed potatoes. Cheese cubes will melt slightly, forming gooey strands in the potato puree.

HASH BROWNS

Hash Browns are a softer, moister version of home fries.

1 tablespoon butter
1 tablespoon oil
4 cups diced cooked potatoes
1 tablespoon grated onion
1 tablespoon chopped parsley
½ teaspoon paprika
¼ cup milk
salt
pepper

Heat fat in a skillet and add potatoes and onion. Cook, stirring occasionally, for 15 minutes.

Add parsley, paprika, and milk. Turn potatoes with a spatula, and cook 5 minutes longer. Season to taste with salt and pepper.

Serves 4

Note: To keep warm until serving, cover pan.

OVEN FRIES

If you don't like frying, but do like fried potatoes, this could be your answer. Oven-frying of potatoes means less oil, fewer calories, less work, less expense, and less mess.

1 pound potatoes
1 tablespoon oil
½ teaspoon paprika

Preheat oven to 450°F.

Scrub but do not peel potatoes. Cut as for french fries into sticks about ⅓ inch wide. Thinner fries can be made for crunchy "potato sticks"; thicker pieces will retain more potato taste and texture.

Toss potato pieces in a bowl with oil to coat. Add paprika and mix well (this enhances the color).

Spread on an oiled baking sheet and bake for 10 minutes. Loosen with a spatula, shake to keep from sticking, and bake 20 to 30 minutes longer. When done the outside will be firm to the touch, but they will be tender inside. The thinner sticks may be done sooner. Shake several times during baking to keep loose.

Serve, seasoning with salt to taste.

Serves 3 to 4

Note: Instead of salting potatoes, sprinkle with grated cheese during the last few minutes of baking. Oven Fries freeze quite successfully. Restore by placing in the broiler for 3 to 5 minutes.

SWEET BAKED SQUASH

Winter squash is naturally sweet and baking brings out its delicate nuttiness.

orange-fleshed winter squash
butter
honey or maple syrup (optional)

Preheat oven to 350° to 375°F.

Cut squash in half lengthwise from stem to blossom end. Scoop out seeds.

Place cut-side down in a shallow baking pan and surround with about ½ inch of water to prevent scorching. Bake for 30 to 40 minutes, or until barely tender.

Invert squash, rub surface with butter, and, if desired, about ½ teaspoon sweetening per half. Return to the oven for 10 to 15 minutes until flesh is tender and cut surface browned.

1 small acorn squash serves 2; a large acorn or hubbard or butternut squash serves 4

Note: A light sprinkling of cinnamon and/or nutmeg can be used for additional seasoning.

STIR-STEAMED VEGETABLES

Steaming vegetables by adding a little liquid to the pan
after stir-frying gives them a more tender texture. The use
of butter makes a rich sauce that needs no seasoning,
allowing you to appreciate the taste of the vegetable.

2 tablespoons butter, or half butter, half oil
1 medium onion, sliced
4 cups thinly sliced vegetables of choice
  (see Variations)
½ cup water

Heat fat in a wok or skillet, add vegetables, and stir-fry
over medium-high heat for 5 to 10 minutes until edges
begin to brown. Add water, cover, reduce heat, and cook 5
to 10 minutes longer until tender.
Serves 4
Variations: This recipe can be prepared with one vegetable or a combination. For *Winter Stir-Steamed Vegetables*,
prepare a mixture of peeled parsnips, peeled turnips, carrots, cauliflower, and leeks.

For *Summer Stir-Steamed Vegetables*, combine young
carrots, zucchini, green beans, fresh corn, and peas. If
desired, add some tomato to the steaming step. If you
prepare vegetables in chunks rather than thin slices, increase the steaming time to about 20 minutes for "summer" vegetables, 30 for "winter" recommendations.

QUICK VEGETABLE MEDLEY

A mosaic of shredded vegetables with your choice of seasonings.

3 cups shredded raw vegetables from the following
   list (include at least two colors):
   potato
   sweet potato
   carrot
   winter squash
   zucchini
   parsnip
   turnip
1 teaspoon salt
½ cup water
1 tablespoon butter
pinch nutmeg, ginger, cumin, curry powder, or soy
   sauce

Combine vegetables, salt, and water in a saucepan. Bring to a boil, cover, reduce heat, and cook for 5 minutes until tender. Season with butter and any of the seasonings you wish.

Serves 6

Note: This medley can be mixed with cooked grains for stuffing vegetables or omelets. Pureed with milk and heated, it becomes a light soup.

HOT DRESSED VEGETABLES

Fresh cooked vegetables in a hot salad dressing.

¾ pound vegetable of choice (broccoli, cauliflower, green beans, beets, potato), cut into manageable pieces
2 tablespoons wine or cider vinegar
¼ cup oil
dash prepared mustard
¼ teaspoon salt
½ teaspoon soy sauce
½ teaspoon dried chervil or 1 tablespoon fresh parsley
1 hard-cooked egg, chopped

Steam vegetables. Combine vinegar, oil, mustard, and salt in a small saucepan and bring to a boil. Remove from heat and beat in soy sauce, herbs, and the egg. Pour warm dressing over hot vegetable in serving dish.

Serves 4

Variation: Use ½ cup prepared oil and vinegar dressing as the base, heating and seasoning as above.

VEGETABLES WITH RICH CRUMB TOPPING

A savory crumb topping can add richness to your favorite vegetables and interest to less favored ones.

1 pound vegetables
1½ cups mixed fresh or dried whole grain bread crumbs, wheat germ, and nut meal
¼ teaspoon salt (optional)
3 tablespoons oil/butter
1 clove garlic, minced (optional)

Steam vegetables until just tender. Make a mixture of crumbs, wheat germ, and nuts, including at least some ground sunflower seeds, soy nuts, or peanuts. Ingredients can be used in any proportion but about half bread crumbs is a good measure. Season with salt if desired.

Heat fat in a 10-inch skillet and cook garlic briefly (if included). Add crumbs and sauté quickly, stirring until crisp and golden. Place vegetables on a serving plate and top with crumbs.

Serves 4
Minor Protein
Note: Vegetables that are especially good this way include leeks, cauliflower, green beans, carrots, sweet potatoes. Many seasonings can be added to the bread crumbs including thyme and sage for a "stuffing" flavor, oregano and basil for Italian vegetables, cinnamon, nutmeg, and ginger for those suited to sweet tastes, and nutritional yeast for just about everything.

REFRIED BEANS

Refried beans, which are a Mexican staple, are really nothing more complicated than precooked beans mashed in hot oil.

2 tablespoons oil
1 small onion, chopped
½ to 1 tablespoon chili powder (optional)
3 cups cooked pinto or kidney beans, drained

Heat oil in a 10- to 12-inch skillet and brown onion lightly. Add chili powder, if desired, and cook for 30 seconds. Add beans and mash with a potato masher or fork until beans are a thick mush. If necessary add a little bean cooking liquid to help soften the mixture. When completely mashed, raise the heat and cook until quite dry.

Serves 4
Protein Complement
Variation: For *Refried Beans with Cheese,* scatter some Jack or cheddar cheese over the beans after mashing, cover pan, and remove from heat to melt.

TWO-TONE MEXICAN BEANS

A two-layer bean dish: one whole and lightly sweetened, the other mashed and spicy. A dollop of yogurt or sour cream on top of the beans is an appropriate garnish.

3 cups cooked kidney or pinto beans, drained
2 tablespoons bean cooking liquid
1 tablespoon molasses
1 tablespoon oil
1 small onion, chopped
1½ teaspoons chili powder

Place half the beans in a saucepan with bean liquid and molasses. Cook over medium heat for about 5 minutes until warm and dry.

Heat oil in a small skillet, brown onion and chili powder, and cook the remaining beans, mashing gently with a fork until thick and dry.

To serve, place some of the mashed beans on each plate. Top with cooked whole beans.

Serves 4
Protein Complement

CHICK-PEAS WITH GRAVY

1 medium onion, chopped
1 clove garlic, chopped
1 tablespoon oil
¼ cup tahini
1 to 2 tablespoons soy sauce
½ cup water or bean cooking liquid
3 cups cooked chick-peas, drained
lemon wedge

Sauté onion and garlic in oil until lightly browned, about 5 minutes over medium-high heat.

Combine tahini, soy sauce, and liquid using only 1 tablespoon soy sauce if liquid is salty, 2 if you are using water. Mix until smooth.

Add tahini mixture and chick-peas to onion and cook over moderate heat, stirring until thick and creamy and just beginning to boil, 3 to 5 minutes.

Squeeze in lemon juice and serve.

Serves 4

Major Protein

VERY QUICK CURRIED CHICK-PEAS

A lightly spiced bean accompaniment.

1 clove garlic, chopped
1 small onion, chopped
1 tablespoon oil
2 teaspoons curry powder
1 cup chopped tomato
3 cups cooked chick-peas, drained

Sauté garlic and onion in oil for 2 to 3 minutes until tender and transparent. Add curry powder and sauté 1 minute longer. Add tomato and chick-peas, cover and cook for about 10 minutes until tomato is soft and beans are hot.

Serves 4

Protein Complement

Note: For a spicier taste, increase curry powder to 1 tablespoon.

COLD TAHINI BEANS

¼ to ⅓ cup water or cooking liquid from beans
2 tablespoons tahini
⅛ teaspoon cayenne
lemon juice
salt (omit if beans are salted)
3 cups cooked chick-peas, white beans, or fava
    beans, drained

Stir liquid gradually into tahini until smooth and of thin
gravy consistency. Add cayenne, a little lemon juice to taste,
and salt (if beans are unsalted). Stir in beans and serve.

Serves 4
Minor Protein
Note: This recipe can be used to improve the flavor of
canned beans.

SPAGHETTI WITH GARLIC

½ pound spaghetti
2 tablespoons olive oil
2 large cloves garlic, chopped
oregano (optional)

Cook spaghetti in boiling salted water for 10 to 12
minutes to taste.

During the last few minutes that pasta cooks, heat oil in a
small heatproof pan or metal measuring cup and cook
garlic until it just colors, about 3 minutes over moderate
heat. Do not overcook.

Drain spaghetti and toss in a serving dish with hot garlic
oil. Sprinkle with a little crushed oregano for added flavor,
if desired. Serve at once.

Serves 4
Protein Complement

CRACKED-WHEAT PILAF

A fast-cooking whole grain.

> 1 cup cracked wheat (sometimes called bulgur)
> 1 small onion, chopped
> 1½ tablespoons oil
> ½ teaspoon salt
> 2 cups water or vegetable broth

Sauté cracked wheat and onion in oil until onion is transparent and wheat glazed. Add salt and liquid and bring to a boil. Cover and cook over low heat for 15 minutes until liquid is absorbed and grain tender. Lift cover partially to let steam escape.

Serves 4

Protein Complement

Note: This recipe allows for ½-cup servings and is meant as a side dish. To serve as a base under a main dish, double the portions.

Variation: For *Mushroom Pilaf,* sauté ¼ pound (1 heavy cup) diced mushrooms along with cracked wheat and onion.

BROWN "RICE-A-RONI"

Rice and pasta cooked together are more than twice as good as each cooked alone.

2 tablespoons butter
½ cup whole wheat spaghetti, broken into 1-inch pieces
1 cup uncooked brown rice
2 cups boiling water
1 tablespoon soy sauce
¼ teaspoon salt

Melt butter in a 2-quart pot, add spaghetti and rice, and sauté for 3 to 5 minutes until golden. Stir frequently and avoid overcooking. Add remaining ingredients, cover, and simmer over low heat until liquid is completely absorbed and grain is tender, about 45 minutes.

Serves 4
Protein Complement

BUTTER NUT GRAINS

To cheer up leftover grains.

1 cup mixed nuts including cashews, peanuts, sunflower and pumpkin seeds
3 cups cooked grains (one or more: brown rice, cracked wheat, kasha, millet)
2 tablespoons butter

In a large ungreased skillet brown nuts over medium heat for 5 to 10 minutes, watching carefully so they do not burn. Add grains; stir briefly, breaking up any clumps with a fork. Dot top with butter, turn heat as low as you can, cover and cook 5 minutes until heated through.

Serves 4 to 6
Minor Protein

OAT PILAF

Very nice with eggs.

2 tablespoons oil
½ cup chopped onion
1½ cups oats
1 egg, lightly beaten
**¾ cup vegetable broth, or water seasoned with
Tomato Cubes (page 246) or tomato juice, or
plain water**
¼ cup chopped parsley
½ teaspoon dried basil
½ teaspoon oregano
¼ teaspoon salt (omit if broth is salted)

Heat oil in a small saucepan and sauté onion for 3 to 5 minutes until tender.

Mix oats with egg, add to onion, and cook, stirring, until each grain is separate and dry.

Add liquid and seasonings; simmer uncovered, stirring a few times, until grain is swollen and tender, about 5 minutes. Cover until ready to serve.

Serves 4

Minor Protein

Variation: For *Oat–Vegetable Pilaf*, add up to ½ cup any or all of the following along with the onion: chopped green or red pepper, mushrooms, celery, or zucchini.

Salads

TANGY COLESLAW

This coleslaw with its light tomato flavor is especially good in Veggie Reubens.

3 to 4 cups finely or coarsely shredded cabbage
¼ teaspoon dry mustard
1 tablespoon lemon juice
2 tablespoons tomato juice
2 tablespoons oil
2 tablespoons mayonnaise

Place cabbage in a bowl. Combine remaining ingredients and mix well with cabbage. If made in advance, chill before serving.
Serves 4

GREEK COLESLAW

The most important requirement in preparing Greek Coleslaw is that you work the shredded vegetable with your hands.

1 clove garlic (optional)
¾ pound cabbage, coarsely shredded (about 4 cups)
juice of ½ lemon

If a little garlic flavor is desired, cut garlic clove and rub it into the salad bowl, then discard. Fill bowl with shredded cabbage and knead with your hands until cabbage softens. Squeeze in lemon juice and toss.
Serves 4

LEMON GREENS

This is the simplest of all salads and very refreshing with a heavy or spicy meal.

   **crisp greens such as romaine, escarole, chicory,
      either singly or mixed
   lemon wedges**

Shred greens coarsely with a knife. Put on a serving plate. Squeeze fresh lemon juice over greens to coat without drowning. Toss. Chill or serve at once.

MARINATED CUCUMBER SALAD

   **2 medium cucumbers, peeled if necessary, and
      sliced thin
   ¼ cup cider vinegar
   2 tablespoons water
   1½ teaspoons honey
   4 thin slices onion
   ¼ teaspoon prepared mustard or 1½ teaspoons
      caraway seeds or 1 tablespoon fresh dill or 1
      teaspoon celery seed**

Toss cucumber with vinegar, water, honey, onion, and seasoning of choice.
   Serves 4 to 6

YOGURT–CUCUMBER SALAD

A versatile salad that goes well with both Mideastern and American cuisines.

1½ cups peeled, thinly sliced cucumber
1 cup yogurt
½ to 1 tablespoon crushed dried mint
dash lemon juice

Gently mix all ingredients, adjusting mint to personal taste. If possible, prepare in advance so flavors have a chance to develop.
Serves 4
Minor Protein
Variations: Cucumber can be grated and pressed to extract moisture for a slightly varied texture. Dried mint can be replaced with 2 to 4 tablespoons fresh mint, or the flavor can be altered entirely by adding parsley, dill, or a little cumin to taste, or by adding 2 thinly sliced scallions.

RICOTTA–CUCUMBER SALAD

This is similar to potato salad in consistency and flavor.

1 cup ricotta cheese
1 medium cucumber, peeled and cubed
2 scallions, thinly sliced
½ teaspoon dried basil
salt
pepper

Combine all ingredients, adding salt if desired and pepper for a little bite. Serve on a bed of lettuce. Garnish with olives and pimientos.
Serves 4
Minor Protein

AMERICAN-STYLE POTATO SALAD

1 pound potatoes, steamed and sliced (about
   3 cups)
¼ cup mayonnaise
¼ cup yogurt
1½ tablespoons wine vinegar
¼ teaspoon salt
pepper
¼ cup chopped scallions
¼ cup chopped sweet green or red pepper
paprika

Cooked potatoes should be at room temperature or chilled. Combine mayonnaise, yogurt, vinegar, salt, and pepper to make a smooth dressing. Add scallion, sweet pepper, and potatoes; stir gently to coat well without breaking up potatoes.

Chill if not for immediate use, but remove about 15 minutes before serving. Sprinkle liberally with paprika.

Serves 4

MACARONI SALAD

A new version that is rich in flavor and protein.

1 cup ricotta cheese
½ cup yogurt
1 teaspoon prepared mustard
4 cups cooked small whole wheat pasta (elbows,
   small shells, spirals)
2 tablespoons chopped green olives
2 tablespoons chopped sweet red or green pepper
2 minced scallions
1 tablespoon minced parsley
salt
pepper

Mix ricotta, yogurt, and mustard until it has a smooth,
mayonnaise-like consistency. If too stiff, add 1 to 2 tablespoons water. Stir pasta and remaining ingredients into
dressing, seasoning to taste with salt and pepper.

Serves 4 to 6
Minor Protein
Note: Cottage cheese can be used instead of ricotta for a
chunky rather than a smooth dressing.

FRENCH PASTA SALAD

A good party choice for buffet dining.

1 can (14 ounces) artichoke hearts in water
3 cups cold, cooked fettucine
¼ cup mayonnaise
¼ cup yogurt
1½ tablespoons tomato juice
capers
fresh chopped parsley

Drain artichokes, rinse under cold water, and drain again. Cut in half and toss with pasta in a serving dish. Mix mayonnaise, yogurt, and tomato juice and pour over pasta just before serving. Garnish with capers and parsley.

Serves 4

Minor Protein

Menu Suggestions: This can also serve as the first course preceding a soufflé or a vegetable entrée.

COLD PASTA WITH TOMATO DRESSING

Prepare with fresh cooked or leftover pasta.

2 large tomatoes, cut into wedges
2 thin slices red onion, cut into quarters
6 sliced olives
2 tablespoons oil
1 tablespoon wine vinegar
½ teaspoon salt
pepper
5 to 6 fresh basil leaves, minced, or 2 tablespoons
**   minced parsley**
1 cup slivered provolone and/or mozzarella cheese
2 cups cooked whole wheat pasta

Combine tomato, onion, olives, oil, vinegar, and seasonings, and mix well. Let stand for a few minutes. Add cheese and pasta to tomato dressing. Serve at room temperature.

Serves 4

Minor Protein

TOFU ANTIPASTO SALAD

In our experience, one of the best ways to serve tofu.

1⅓ cups sliced mushrooms
1 cup sliced celery
1½ cups tomato chunks
½ cup small strips green pepper
1½ cups diced tofu
¼ cup lemon juice
6 tablespoons oil (part olive preferred)
1½ teaspoons oregano
½ teaspoon salt
pepper

Combine all vegetables and tofu. Pour on lemon juice, oil and seasonings. Mix gently to combine. Marinate at room temperature for 30 minutes, or longer in the refrigerator. Adjust salt and pepper to taste before serving.
Serves 6
Minor Protein

AVOCADO COCKTAIL

2 small to medium avocados
1 cup Spicy Tomato Dressing and Cocktail
   Marinade (recipe on page 157)
shredded lettuce or alfalfa sprouts

Peel avocado and cut in cubes. Mix with dressing and marinate at least 30 minutes. Serve on individual plates on bed of shredded lettuce or mound of alfalfa sprouts.
Serves 4

MUSHROOM COCKTAIL

½ pound mushrooms
1 cup Spicy Tomato Dressing and Cocktail
   Marinade (recipe follows)
shredded lettuce or alfalfa sprouts

Clean mushrooms. If small, leave whole; cut into halves or quarters if large. Pieces should be of substantial size. Mix with dressing and marinate at least 30 minutes. Serve on individual plates on bed of shredded lettuce or mound of alfalfa sprouts.
Serves 4

SPICY TOMATO DRESSING AND COCKTAIL MARINADE

½ cup tomato juice
¼ teaspoon hot pepper sauce
2 tablespoons minced onion
½ clove garlic
¼ teaspoon salt
2 tablespoons wine vinegar
¼ cup oil (at least part olive preferred)

Combine all ingredients. Use for appetizer service (as in recipes above) or as a salad dressing.
Makes 1 cup

COLD EGGPLANT AND YOGURT

A cool dish that provides contrast to a spicy entrée.

  1 medium eggplant (1 to 1½ pounds)
  4 scallions, sliced
  ½ teaspoon salt
  2 tablespoons minced parsley
  3 tablespoons oil
  4 tablespoons lemon juice
  ¼ cup sliced olives
  1 cup yogurt

Peel eggplant, cut in 1-inch cubes, and steam for about 7 minutes until just tender but not mushy. Cool slightly.

Toss eggplant in a bowl with scallions, salt, parsley, oil, lemon juice, and olives. Mix well, cover, and let stand at room temperature for 30 minutes, or chill for several hours.

Stir in yogurt just before serving.

Serves 4 to 6
Minor Protein

CARROT–PEANUT SALAD

  4 good-sized carrots, grated (about 2½ cups)
  ½ cup peanuts, finely chopped
  3 tablespoons yogurt
  3 tablespoons mayonnaise

Combine all ingredients and mix well. Serve as is or on a bed of mixed shredded greens.

Serves 4
Minor Protein

Dressings and Sauces

BOTTOM-OF-THE-BOWL DRESSING

If you don't care about having extra dressing to store, the easiest approach to salad making is to prepare the dressing in the bottom of the bowl. The greens and vegetables are placed on top, and the salad is tossed just before eating to bring up the dressing and coat the vegetables.

For a salad for one:

Squeeze juice of ½ small lemon in the bottom of a bowl. Dip the tip of a clean fork into your favorite prepared mustard and beat lemon juice around the bowl with this fork.

Gradually beat in about 1 tablespoon oil so that dressing becomes creamy and spreads around bottom and slightly up sides of the bowl. Taste and adjust with salt, pepper, and more oil or lemon to taste. If desired, add some chervil, parsley, basil, or other favorite seasoning. When dressing is to your taste, prepare the salad.

For a salad for two:

Use ½ medium to large lemon, dip deeper into the mustard, and increase the oil proportionately. Double this recipe to serve up to 4. For larger servings, the dressing is best made in a separate container.

BASIC OIL AND VINEGAR DRESSING

The classic proportion of oil to vinegar is 3 to 1. We prefer a ratio closer to 2 to 1, which is less delicate but more flavorful.

¼ cup wine or cider vinegar
¼ teaspoon salt
dash Dijon mustard
pepper
½ to ¾ cup oil

Using a fork or wire whisk, beat vinegar with salt, mustard, and pepper. Gradually beat in oil until the dressing is slightly creamy and diluted to taste. Dressing ingredients can also be combined in a jar and shaken together in lieu of beating, but the gradual addition of oil makes a creamier dressing.

Makes ¾ to 1 cup dressing

Note: Substituting fresh lemon juice for some of the vinegar produces a mellower dressing. Substituting all lemon juice imparts a distinct lemon taste. If the dressing is too sharp and you do not wish to add more oil, it can be diluted with a little water.

Variations: For *Garlic Dressing*, add 1 minced clove garlic.

For *Herb Dressing*, add ½ teaspoon dried chervil, ¼ teaspoon dried or 1 tablespoon fresh basil, 1 tablespoon fresh dill or parsley, using any one or several in combination. A split clove of garlic can also be added.

For *Italian Dressing*, add a split clove of garlic and ¼ teaspoon each dried basil and oregano. Use wine vinegar and at least part olive oil.

For *Creamy Dressing*, beat in up to 3 tablespoons yogurt.

For *Soft Cheese Dressing*, beat in 3 tablespoons crumbled feta or blue cheese.

For *Rich Parsley Dressing*, combine ¼ cup parsley with

the vinegar and seasonings in a blender or processor fitted with a steel blade. With the motor running, add oil in a steady stream through the feeder cap until dressing is creamy and parsley is finely minced.

For *Chunky Cottage Cheese Dressing*, add 1 tablespoon minced parsley, 1 minced scallion, and ¼ cup cottage cheese. Shake well so that ingredients are well distributed but tiny lumps of cheese remain. This is especially good on tomato salads and mixed greens.

REVISIONIST DRESSING

This is the American Wholefoods version of Russian dressing.

⅓ cup mayonnaise
⅔ cup yogurt
½ cup tomato juice
1 teaspoon soy sauce
¼ teaspoon hot pepper sauce

Combine all ingredients and mix until smooth.
Makes 1½ cups
Minor Protein

FRENCH TOMATO VINAIGRETTE

½ tablespoon tomato paste
2 tablespoons wine vinegar
6 tablespoons oil

Beat all ingredients with a fork until smooth.
Makes ½ cup dressing
Variations: For *Creamy French Tomato Vinaigrette*, beat in ¼ cup yogurt.

For *Italian Tomato Vinaigrette*, add ¼ teaspoon dried basil and ⅛ teaspoon oregano.

For *Mexican Tomato Vinaigrette*, replace wine vinegar with cider vinegar and add ½ teaspoon chili powder.

LIGHT FRENCH TOMATO DRESSING

This is a very pleasing dressing with only one third the calories of standard salad dressings.

½ cup tomato juice
2 tablespoons wine vinegar
¼ cup olive oil
1 clove garlic, split
¼ teaspoon salt
1 tablespoon minced fresh parsley or 1 teaspoon
   dried chervil
pepper
½ teaspoon honey

Combine all ingredients in a jar and shake to mix.
Makes 1 cup
Variations: For *Light Italian Tomato Dressing*, add ½ teaspoon dried oregano, ½ teaspoon dried basil, and a dash of hot pepper sauce.

For *Light Mexican Tomato Dressing*, replace some or all of the vinegar with fresh lemon or lime juice. Add 1 teaspoon chili powder and ¼ teaspoon hot pepper sauce.

NO-OIL TOMATO JUICE DRESSING

Appropriate for those who want a fat-free dressing. To accommodate those who want a richer or more traditional dressing, serve a separate cruet of oil. Once the salad is dressed and served, oil can be added to taste.

½ cup tomato juice
2 tablespoons lemon juice
½ teaspoon honey
1 teaspoon celery seed, or 1 tablespoon chopped
   chives
pepper

Mix ingredients together, using a generous amount of pepper.

Makes ⅔ cup dressing; serves 4

THICK CREAMY BLUE CHEESE DRESSING

½ cup yogurt
2 tablespoons mayonnaise
¼ cup crumbled blue or Roquefort cheese

Combine all ingredients and mix well.
Makes ¾ cup
Minor Protein

CREAMY TOFU GARLIC DRESSING

The East–West restaurant in New York City served a salad with a dressing like this one that was so delicious it was not unusual for people to order two at a single sitting.

8 ounces tofu (1 large or 2 small squares)
2 tablespoons cider vinegar
1 tablespoon lemon juice
¼ teaspoon dry mustard
pinch salt
1 tablespoon soy sauce
1 clove garlic, minced
¼ cup oil
about ⅓ cup water

Combine tofu, vinegar, lemon juice, mustard, salt, soy sauce, and garlic in a blender or a processor fitted with a plastic or steel blade. Puree until smooth. With machine running, add oil through feeder. Gradually add water until dressing is of thick pouring consistency.
Makes 1 cup dressing; serves 6 to 8
Minor Protein

WHIPPED COTTAGE CREAM

Use on potato pancakes, baked potatoes, tacos, enchiladas, and anything else you might use sour cream on. This dressing is low in fat and calories and high in protein.

1 cup cottage cheese
1 tablespoon yogurt or milk, as needed
dash lemon juice

Puree cottage cheese until smooth in a processor fitted with a plastic blade or in a blender. Add yogurt or milk, if needed, to get the blender moving. If you have neither machine, cottage cheese can be pureed in a food mill or pressed through a sieve, then thinned by beating in the yogurt or milk with a fork or wire whisk. Season to taste with a little lemon juice for a "sour" effect.

Makes 1 cup
Minor Protein

FRESH MAYONNAISE

Once you are accustomed to having fresh mayonnaise, it's hard to go back to the store-bought kind.

1 egg
½ teaspoon dry mustard
½ tablespoon lemon juice
½ teaspoon salt
1 cup oil (safflower or sunflower preferred)

Break egg into a deep bowl and put mustard on top. Beat in lemon juice, using a fork or wire whisk. Beat in salt.

Beat in oil in a slow, steady stream without stopping until mayonnaise thickens, or "grabs." This is easiest to do with two people, one to beat and one to pour. Keep chilled and use within a month.

Makes 1 cup

Note: For *Fresh Mayonnaise in a Machine*, combine egg, mustard, lemon juice, and salt in a blender or a processor fitted with a plastic mixing blade. Add ¼ cup oil all at once, blend, and then add remaining oil in a slow, steady stream through the feeder cap until it becomes mayonnaise.

Variation: Mayonnaise can be made with yolks only, replacing each whole egg with two yolks.

TOFU MAYONNAISE

A thick, creamy dressing made with tofu can be seasoned in the same manner as traditional mayonnaise and used to dress salad greens or to bind salad ingredients. The great advantage of this dressing is that it is lower in fat and calories and adds protein to the salad.

½ pound tofu (1 large or 2 small cakes)
2 tablespoons lemon juice or cider vinegar
½ teaspoon salt
¼ teaspoon prepared mustard
3 tablespoons oil
2 to 4 tablespoons water

Pat tofu dry with a paper towel and combine in a blender or a processor fitted with a steel blade with lemon juice, salt, and mustard. Process until creamy. With machine running, add oil through feeder cap, then water, until mayonnaise is of desired consistency.

Makes 1 cup

Minor Protein

Variation: For *Tofu Sour Cream*, omit mustard and water to make a thicker dressing. Increase tartness, if you wish, by stirring in another tablespoon of lemon juice.

CASHEW MAYONNAISE

Nuts, rather than egg, hold this dressing together.

> 2 tablespoons sunflower seeds
> 2 tablespoons cashew pieces
> ¼ cup water
> 2 tablespoons lemon juice
> ¼ cup oil (olive preferred)
> ¼ teaspoon salt

Grind nuts to a powder in a blender or processor. Add water and lemon juice and puree until smooth. With machine running, slowly pour in oil until dressing is thick. Season with salt, adjusting to taste.

Makes about ⅔ cup
Protein Complement

BROWNED ONION RELISH

Use this as a garnish for burgers, egg dishes, or even a baked potato.

> 2 medium onions cut into ¼-inch dice
> ½ tablespoon paprika
> 1 tablespoon oil
> 1 tablespoon soy sauce

Toss onions with paprika in a large skillet until evenly colored. Pour oil over onions and stir to coat. Add soy sauce, place over low heat, cover, and cook for 15 minutes until tender. Stir occasionally. Serve warm or at room temperature.

Serves 2 to 3
Note: Refrigerate leftovers.

TOUCH-OF-HONEY CATSUP

This quick homemade catsup has only ½ tablespoon of sweetening per half cup in the form of honey, as compared to 2½ to 3 tablespoons sugar and/or corn syrup in commercial varieties.

6 tablespoons tomato paste
2 tablespoons lemon juice or cider vinegar
½ teaspoon soy sauce
1½ teaspoons honey
1 tablespoon water

Mix all ingredients together until smooth. Store in the refrigerator for long-term use.

Makes about ½ cup

QUICK BARBECUE SAUCE

A sauce for burgers, bean balls, plain beans, grains, or tofu.

1 small onion, chopped
1 small clove garlic, chopped
2 tablespoons oil
1 tablespoon chili powder
2 teaspoons honey
2 teaspoons prepared mustard
1½ cups tomato juice
2 tablespoons lemon juice

Sauté onion and garlic in oil for about 3 minutes until softened. Add chili powder and cook briefly. Add remaining ingredients, bring to a boil, and simmer, uncovered, for 5 to 10 minutes until slightly thickened.

Makes 1½ cups; serves 4

RAW CREOLE SAUCE

This spicy tomato relish can be served as a garnish on rice, burgers, beans, or any plain vegetable.

    1 pound ripe tomatoes, cut into pieces
    1 teaspoon peeled, coarsely chopped fresh ginger
    2 tablespoons cut-up onion
    ¼ teaspoon cayenne
    2 teaspoons lemon juice

Combine all ingredients in a blender or processor fitted with a steel blade. Blend to an even but coarse texture. Serve at room temperature. Refrigerate for storage and use within a few days.

Makes 2 cups; serves 4 to 6

LIGHT FRESH TOMATO SAUCE

A delicate sauce for pasta or burgers.

    2 tablespoons oil
    2 medium onions, chopped
    1 green pepper, chopped
    2 pounds tomatoes, diced, undrained (about 5½
      cups)
    1½ teaspoons salt
    1 teaspoon honey

Heat oil in a 1½- to 2-quart pot. Cook onion and green pepper until onion becomes translucent. Add tomatoes, salt, and honey and cook over moderate heat for 15 to 20 minutes until tender but not falling apart.

Makes about 1 quart; serves 8

Note: For use on bean burgers, sauce can be sweetened with 1 to 2 teaspoons molasses for a pleasing contrast.

EMERGENCY MEXICAN TOMATO SAUCE

A last-minute sauce for use on enchiladas, tacos, etc.

½ small onion, chopped
1 clove garlic, chopped
2 teaspoons minced hot chili pepper or ¼ teaspoon
   cayenne
1 tablespoon oil
1 tablespoon chili powder
3 cups tomato juice or puree

Sauté onion, garlic, and hot pepper in oil for about 3 minutes until they just begin to color. Add chili powder (and cayenne, if you are using that instead of chili pepper) and cook briefly. Stir in tomato juice and simmer, uncovered, for 5 to 10 minutes until sauce is slightly thickened.
Makes 3 cups

QUICK MEXICAN HOT SAUCE

To be used in small amounts to add flavor and heat to beans, enchiladas, eggs, tacos, chili rellenos, etc., which may already have a milder sauce.

1 tablespoon minced onion
½ small clove garlic, minced
1-inch piece hot chili powder, minced, or
   ⅛ teaspoon or more cayenne
1 tablespoon oil
½ tablespoon chili powder
¾ cup tomato juice
1 tablespoon lemon juice

Sauté onion, garlic, and hot pepper in oil for about 3 minutes until just beginning to color. Add chili powder (and cayenne if you are using that instead of chili pepper) and cook 1 minute longer. Add tomato juice and lemon juice and simmer, uncovered, for 5 to 10 minutes until slightly thickened. Use warm or cold.

Makes ⅔ cup (enough for 6 as a seasoning)

Note: Can be stored in a covered container in the refrigerator for up to 2 weeks.

15-MINUTE ITALIAN TOMATO SAUCE

A quick topping for bean balls, pasta, eggplant, and hot hero sandwiches.

    1 clove garlic, minced
    1 medium green pepper, cut into thin 1-inch pieces
    1 tablespoon oil (olive preferred)
    1½ cups tomato juice or puree
    1 tablespoon tomato paste
    ½ teaspoon oregano
    ½ teaspoon dried basil

Sauté garlic and pepper in oil for about 3 minutes until garlic begins to color. Stir in remaining ingredients, bring to a boil, and simmer uncovered for 10 minutes.

Makes 1½ cups; serves 2

Variations: Add ½ to 1 cup sliced mushrooms with peppers. For *Chunky Pasta Sauce*, add a chopped onion with the green pepper and 1 cup coarsely chopped cooked kidney beans to the remaining ingredients.

Note: Leftover tomato paste can be stored in ice cube trays in the freezer. Measure out 2 tablespoons per cube. Use without defrosting.

PEANUT BUTTER–VEGETABLE SAUCE

Serve over raw or cooked vegetables, especially carrots, broccoli, beets, green beans, or baked sweet or white potatoes. Unlikely as the combination may seem, it is extremely tasty.

½ cup yogurt, or 6 tablespoons yogurt plus
   2 tablespoons sour cream
2 tablespoons peanut butter
2 teaspoons prepared mustard
dash fresh lemon juice

Gradually stir yogurt into peanut butter until well blended; add remaining ingredients.
Makes about ⅔ cup; serves 2 to 4
Minor Protein

YOGURT–TAHINI SAUCE

A slight variation on the standard falafel sauce, this one can be used in its place or spooned over plain cooked beans stuffed into pita pockets.

2 tablespoons lemon juice
¼ teaspoon salt
¼ cup tahini
¼ cup water
½ cup yogurt
1 small clove garlic, crushed
⅓ teaspoon cumin

Beat lemon juice and salt into tahini with a fork until thick. Slowly beat in water until mixture loosens and turns creamy white. Stir in yogurt and seasonings. Sauce will resemble thin mayonnaise in consistency.

Makes 1 cup; serves 4
Minor Protein

DOUBLE CHEESE SAUCE

Excellent on rarebits and vegetables, this cheese sauce has no starch thickener, less milk, about twice the cheese, and is much quicker to prepare than the traditional sauce.

1 tablespoon butter
2 cups shredded cheese, mostly cheddar mixed with
   some Edam, Muenster, or Jack for a mellow
   flavor
½ cup milk
¾ teaspoon prepared mustard
1½ teaspoons soy sauce
⅛ teaspoon cayenne

Melt butter in a small saucepan set on a heatproof pad or in top of a double boiler. Add cheese and stir with a wire whisk until it begins to melt. Gradually stir in milk and seasonings and cook, continuing to stir, until creamy and heated through. Be sure to keep heat extremely low and do not boil.

Makes 1½ cups; serves 4
Major Protein

Quick Bread Baking

BASIC BISCUITS

Our version of one of the oldest American foods.

2 cups whole wheat flour
¼ cup wheat germ
4 teaspoons baking powder
½ teaspoon salt
¼ cup oil
1 tablespoon honey or molasses
about ⅔ cup milk

Preheat oven to 425°F.

Combine dry ingredients. Stir in oil until mixture is crumbly. Add sweetening and enough milk to make a soft dough.

Pat or roll dough gently until it is ½ inch thick. Cut into 2-inch squares or rounds. Reshape outtakes. Place on a baking sheet or pan wiped with oil, leaving an inch between for crusty biscuits; have sides touching for a tender crust. Bake for about 15 minutes until browned.

Makes 10 to 12 biscuits

Minor Protein

Notes: To cut biscuit dough, use an empty food tin or a glass of the desired diameter. For a smooth edge, dip in flour first. Recombine outtakes. Alternately, to eliminate rerolling and to speed production, cut biscuit dough into squares, using a knife dipped in flour.

To freeze unbaked biscuit dough conveniently, cut rolled dough with empty frozen-juice concentrate cans that have both ends removed. Fit rounds gently into cans, cover ends with foil, and freeze. To use, push dough out from one end, break apart, and bake. If still frozen at baking, increase baking time by about 5 minutes. Use dough within two weeks.

Prebaked frozen biscuits can be restored by unwrapping and baking on an oiled pan in a warm (300° to 325°F.) oven for 15 to 20 minutes. Use a toaster oven when defrosting a few biscuits at a time.

Variations: For *Cottage Cheese Biscuits*, reduce milk to about ½ cup and gently knead 1 cup cottage cheese into dough.

For *Soy Biscuits*, replace 1 cup whole wheat flour with 1 cup soy flour, omit wheat germ, and use ½ cup water instead of the milk.

For *Yogurt Biscuits*, reduce baking powder to 2 teaspoons, add ½ teaspoon baking soda, and replace milk with yogurt.

WHEAT GERM MUFFINS

Our favorite all-purpose muffin.

1½ cups whole wheat flour
1 cup wheat germ
½ teaspoon salt
3 teaspoons baking powder
6 tablespoons nonfat dry milk powder
1 cup water
1 egg, lightly beaten
3 tablespoons oil
2 tablespoons honey

Preheat oven to 400°F.

Combine dry ingredients. Make a well in the center, add liquid ingredients, and stir to moisten. Batter will be quite thick. Spoon into oiled muffin cups, filling ¾ for medium muffins, to top for large ones. Bake for 20 to 25 minutes.

Makes 10 to 12 muffins
Minor Protein
Note: For a sweet muffin, increase honey to ¼ cup.

WHOLE WHEAT MUFFINS

2 cups whole wheat flour
2 tablespoons wheat germ
½ teaspoon salt
3 teaspoons baking powder
6 tablespoons nonfat dry milk powder
3 tablespoons oil
1 egg, lightly beaten
1 cup water
¼ cup honey

Preheat oven to 400°F.

Combine dry ingredients. Make a well in the center and add the liquid ingredients. Stir just enough to moisten. Spoon batter into oiled muffin cups, filling ⅔ for medium muffins and almost to the top for large ones. Bake for 15 to 20 minutes.

Makes 12 medium or 9 large muffins

Minor Protein

Variations: Add ¼ cup raisins, chopped dates, and/or nuts to batter.

To make *Corn Muffins*, replace 1 cup whole wheat flour with 1 cup cornmeal; omit wheat germ.

For *Cheese Muffins*, add ½ cup grated sharp cheddar cheese and ⅛ teaspoon cayenne to flour mixture. Reduce honey to 2 tablespoons.

HOUSE CORN BREAD

We like this recipe so well we have repeated it in all of our books.

1 tablespoon butter
1 tablespoon oil
¾ cup cornmeal
1 egg, lightly beaten
½ teaspoon baking soda
½ teaspoon salt
1½ cups yogurt
1 tablespoon honey

Preheat oven to 425°F.

Combine butter and oil in a 9-inch baking pan or a shallow 1-quart casserole. Place in the oven for 5 minutes to melt.

Mix remaining ingredients together and pour into the hot baking dish. Return to the oven for 30 minutes until set. Cut into 3-inch squares to serve.

Makes nine 3-inch pieces

Minor Protein

Note: To double the recipe, use a 9 × 13-inch pan.

Variation: For *Savory Onion Corn Bread*, omit honey, increase salt to ¾ teaspoon, and add ⅓ cup chopped onion to the batter.

SWEET CORN MUFFINS

A sweet muffin with a cakelike crumb. Good enough to serve for dessert.

2½ cups cornmeal
1 tablespoon baking powder
¼ teaspoon salt
⅓ cup oil
⅓ cup honey
1½ cups milk

Preheat oven to 375°F.

Combine dry ingredients. Make a well in the center and add oil, honey, and milk. Stir until batter is smooth. Pour into an oiled muffin tin, filling almost to the top. Bake for 20 to 25 minutes.

Makes 12 muffins
Minor Protein

Variations: For crunchy *Golden Temple Muffins,* fashioned after the millet-flecked muffins served in the Golden Temple of Conscious Cookery Restaurants, add ¼ cup uncooked millet to the batter.

For *Double Corn Muffins,* reduce honey to 3 tablespoons for a less sweet muffin and add ½ cup corn to the batter.

CHAPATIS

A soft, freckled Indian bread.

1 cup whole wheat flour
¼ teaspoon salt
1 tablespoon oil
¼ cup water

Combine flour and salt in a mixing bowl. Work in oil, using your fingers. Pour in water and blend with fingers, kneading until dough holds together. If flour begins to crumble, add a tablespoon of water. You should not have to add more than 2 additional tablespoons.

When dough holds in one mass, place on a work surface wiped with oil and knead for a full 10 minutes until smooth and elastic like clay.

Cover with a damp cloth or invert a mixing bowl over the dough; let stand at room temperature for about 30 minutes, if possible, before rolling. This makes rolling easier.

Divide into six balls. Roll from center out, keeping as round as possible, into a thin 6-inch circle. Continue for all balls, keeping unrolled dough and rolled chapatis covered to prevent drying.

Heat a large, heavy skillet or griddle, or cook on top of a wood-burning stove. When hot, place chapati on the ungreased surface and cook for about 1 minute until bread puffs up slightly in places and bottom is lightly colored. Turn and cook other side until spotted with brown. If necessary, chapati can be turned several times until well freckled. Pressing lightly with a spatula during cooking will make chapatis puff.

As each chapati is removed from the cooking surface, stack and wrap in a cloth napkin or towel to keep warm and pliable. Serve warm, as soon after cooking as possible.

Makes 6 breads; serves 3 to 6

Protein Complement

Note: Prepared chapati dough can be divided into balls and stored in a covered container in the refrigerator.

Variations: For *Spiced Chapatis*, add ¼ teaspoon cayenne, ¼ teaspoon cumin, and ¼ teaspoon turmeric.

Rye Chapatis can be made by substituting rye flour.

REFRESHING TECHNIQUES FOR BREAD, ROLLS, BISCUITS, MUFFINS, ETC.

Place on a steaming basket set in a pot with an inch of boiling water. Cover and steam for one minute.

or

Dampen a brown paper bag with water. Place breadstuff inside. Bake in 350°F. oven until the bag is dry.

Convenience-Mix Recipes

Cooking from a mix is really nothing more than arriving in the kitchen after the ingredients have been put together but before they have been cooked. When time is short, mixes can be a great convenience, and for those cooks who are a bit uncomfortable with certain procedures, a mix lends the confidence and freedom to prepare a sauce or baked goods when they might otherwise hesitate to do so. We suggest, too, that if you have friends who appreciate good food, an extra mix is a thoughtful personal gift.

WHITE SAUCE MIX

White Sauce Mix makes foolproof gravy in less than 10 minutes. The combination of vegetable leftovers and a container of sauce mix in a pantry can be the source of many delicious casseroles and pot pies.

   1 cup whole wheat flour
   2½ cups nonfat dry milk powder
   1 tablespoon salt

Combine all ingredients. Store in a covered container at room temperature. Shake well before each use to distribute ingredients evenly.

Makes 3 cups mix

QUICK WHITE SAUCE

Thin sauce = 3 tablespoons White Sauce Mix
   plus 1 cup milk, water, or a combination
Medium Sauce = ⅓ cup White Sauce Mix plus
   1 cup water or equal parts milk and water
Thick Sauce = ⅔ cup White Sauce Mix plus 1
   cup water

Combine dry mix with enough of the liquid to make a smooth paste. Stir in remaining liquid and cook over moderate heat, continuing to stir frequently until sauce thickens and comes to a boil. Boil gently for 1 to 2 minutes.

Makes 1 cup

Minor Protein

Note: For a richer sauce, add ½ to 1 tablespoon butter per cup of sauce at the end of cooking and stir to melt.

Variations: For *Quick Cheese Sauce,* stir ½ cup grated cheese into 1 cup medium white sauce until melted.

For *Quick Tomato—Cheese Sauce,* prepare medium white sauce, using ¼ cup water to form the paste and ¾ cup tomato juice for the remaining liquid. After sauce has thickened stir in ½ cup shredded cheese to melt. A combination of cheddar and mozzarella cheeses is particularly good.

For *Quick Creamed Soups,* make a paste of ¾ cup mix and ½ cup water and stir gradually into 1 quart hot broth or soup stock of choice. Boil gently for 2 minutes.

For a homey cup of *Quick Cream of Tomato Soup,* combine 3 tablespoons mix with ¼ cup milk to make a smooth paste. Gradually stir in ¾ cup tomato juice and cook as usual.

MUSHROOM SAUCE MIX

"Prep" this mix for mushroom sauce on demand.

½ ounce (about ⅔ cup) dried mushrooms
1 cup whole wheat flour
2½ cups nonfat dry milk powder
1 tablespoon salt
1 teaspoon nutmeg
2 tablespoons nutritional yeast

Crush half the mushrooms until quite small and leave the remainder as they come.

Combine all ingredients and store in a covered container at room temperature. Mix thoroughly before each use.

Makes 3¾ cups mix

QUICK MUSHROOM SAUCE

Medium sauce = 6 tablespoons Mushroom Sauce
Mix plus 1 cup water
Thick sauce = ¾ cup Mushroom Sauce Mix plus
1 cup water

Combine dry mix with some of the water to make a smooth paste, using about ¼ cup liquid to each 6 tablespoons mix. Add remaining water and stir continuously over moderate heat until sauce thickens and comes to a boil. Boil gently for 1 to 2 minutes to cook out the raw flour taste.

Makes 1 cup
Minor Protein
Variation: For a *Tangy Quick Mushroom Sauce,* prepare 1 cup medium sauce, remove from heat and stir in 1 tablespoon each yogurt and sour cream. If reheating is necessary, keep heat low and do not boil.

POCKET SOUP MIX

Those who enjoy an instant cup of broth but are dismayed by the use of flavor enhancers and the abundance of salt in commercial brands may welcome the chance to make their own soup mix.

2 tablespoons dried split peas
2 tablespoons cracked wheat
¼ cup dehydrated vegetable flakes (soup greens)
2 teaspoons sesame seeds
2 teaspoons sunflower seeds
1 teaspoon nutritional yeast
½ teaspoon salt

Grind split peas, cracked wheat, vegetable flakes, and seeds in blender until they are a fine powder. Combine ground mixture with yeast and salt. Store in a covered container at room temperature.

To use, add 1 heaping teaspoon soup mix to 6 ounces boiling water, or 2 level teaspoons to 1 cup boiling water. Stir, let sit a few minutes, and serve.

Makes ¾ cup dried soup mix (enough for 18 cups of soup)

Note: This is one of those times when the blender seems to do a much more efficient job than the food processor.

BURGER MIX

There are several good commercial mixes, but you may prefer to make your own, thereby reducing the cost of your meal.

½ cup dried chick-peas
¼ cup dried soybeans
¼ cup dried lentils
¼ cup peanuts
¼ cup sunflower seeds
¼ cup sesame seeds
¼ cup oats
¼ cup cornmeal
¼ cup wheat germ
2 tablespoons soy flour
1 tablespoon nutritional yeast
2 tablespoons dried parsley
1 teaspoon baking soda
1½ teaspoons salt

Grind the beans, nuts, seeds, and oats in the blender to consistency of coarse flour. For best results, process only ½ cup at a time. Combine mixture with remaining ingredients and mix well to distribute evenly. Store in a covered container at cool room temperature or refrigerate.

Makes 4 cups (enough for 8 burgers or 24 fritters)

Note: If you do not have the beans called for, others can be used as long as you have a total of 1 cup dried beans to begin with. Nuts and grains can also be varied with others in equal quantity. Cracked wheat, barley, rice, or millet can all be ground in the blender until they are a suitable texture.

BURGER MIX BURGERS

A delicious and tender burger that you can pan-fry or cook on the grill to enjoy on a bun or just by itself on a plate.

> 1 cup Burger Mix (recipe page 184)
> ⅓ cup hot water
> dash soy sauce

Combine Burger Mix with water and a little soy sauce; mix well and let stand about 15 minutes to absorb the moisture. Shape into 2 patties.

Heat a heavy skillet and cover with a thin layer of oil. When hot, add burgers and cook 3 to 5 minutes or until bottom is brown. Turn, cover pan, and cook about 5 minutes longer, steaming the interior and browning the bottom at the same time.

Serves 1

Major Protein

Variations: For grilled burgers, place on a rack over hot coals and brown each side. For *Burger Mix Fritters,* form mixture into 6 balls and deep-fry in skillet or wok. These can be stuffed into pita pockets with salad and dressing and served like falafel.

Multipurpose Flour Mixes

Although muffins, biscuits, pancakes, and the like are not difficult to prepare from scratch, knowing that most of the measuring and mixing has already taken place is both psychologically encouraging and time-saving.

On the following pages are three of our favorite mixes, and recipes using them. All should be stored in the refrigerator and used within three months for best results.

As directed in the recipes, the mix should be spooned lightly into the measure without compressing.

EXTRA LIGHT MIX

This particular mix gives a tender product with only the faintest trace of wheat flavor.

4 cups whole wheat flour
1 cup nonfat dry milk powder
2½ tablespoons baking powder
1½ teaspoons salt
½ cup oil

In a large bowl, blender, or processor fitted with a plastic mixing blade, combine the dry ingredients and mix well. Slowly add oil, mixing continually until it is completely absorbed.

Store in a closed container in the refrigerator and mix well before each use.

Makes about 7 cups; 1¾ pounds

QUICK LIGHT BISCUITS

2¼ cups Extra Light Mix, spooned into measure
½ cup water

Preheat oven to 425°F.

Add water to mix to form an even dough. Knead gently to combine. Pat into a rectangle ½ inch thick. Cut into eight 2-inch squares.

Bake for 15 to 20 minutes until golden. Serve while still warm.

Makes 8 biscuits
Minor Protein

QUICK LIGHT MUFFINS

3 cups Extra Light Mix, spooned into measure
1 cup water
1 egg, beaten
2 tablespoons honey

Preheat oven to 400°F.
Combine all ingredients and stir gently until completely
moistened.
Spoon into an oiled muffin tin, filling each cup two-
thirds full. Bake for 15 to 20 minutes.
Makes 8 muffins
Minor Protein

QUICK LIGHT PANCAKES

1¾ cups Extra Light Mix, spooned into measure
1 cup water
1 egg, beaten
1 tablespoon honey

Combine all ingredients and stir gently until completely
moistened. Drop by quarter cupfuls onto a hot pan that
has been wiped with oil.
Cook until bottom is lightly browned and spatula slips
underneath with ease. Flip and cook until bottom is set and
freckled.
Makes 10 pancakes; serves 2
Minor Protein

QUICK BREADSTICKS

These can be kept in a covered container and will surely be consumed before they have a chance to stale.

2½ cups Extra Light Mix, spooned into measure
½ cup cornmeal
½ cup water
3 to 4 tablespoons sesame seeds

Preheat oven to 400°F.

Combine mix and cornmeal in a bowl. Add water and stir to form a dough that holds together. Knead gently with mixture still in bowl in order to get dough to stick. If too dry, add a little water as needed.

Pinch off dough in small balls, about 1½ inches in diameter. Roll between your palms, pressing gently into "cigars" ½ inch wide and about 3½ inches long. Moisten sticks lightly with wet hands and roll in sesame seeds to cover.

Place on an oiled baking sheet and bake for about 20 minutes, or until golden. Serve warm, or cool completely and eat at room temperature.

Makes 16 breadsticks
Minor Protein

QUICK POT PIE

Transform leftovers into something more exciting to eat.

6 cups cooked beans, vegetables, or other leftovers
in gravy.
1½ cups Extra Light Mix, spooned into measure
½ cup water
1 tablespoon honey (optional)

Preheat oven to 400°F.

Place mixture to be covered in a 1½- to 2-quart casse-

CONVENIENCE-MIX RECIPES · 189

role or deep 9½- to 10-inch pie plate. Pan should be about three-fourths full.

Combine mix with water and honey and stir gently until well moistened. Drop batter by spoonfuls evenly on top of baking dish.

Bake for 15 to 20 minutes until nicely browned.

Serves 4

Minor Protein or *Major Protein*, depending on filling used.

CHEESE PIE

A simplified quiche of sorts, in which the batter sinks to form a crust and the cheese custard rises to the top.

paprika
1 cup shredded Swiss cheese
½ cup chopped onion
3 eggs
1½ cups milk
½ cup Extra Light Mix, spooned into measure
½ teaspoon prepared mustard

Preheat oven to 325°F.

Generously butter a 9-inch pie pan and sprinkle with about ¼ teaspoon paprika. Arrange cheese and onion in the pan.

Beat eggs with milk, mix, and mustard until smooth. Pour over cheese. Sprinkle evenly with paprika.

Bake for about 30 minutes, or until set. Let stand for 10 minutes before serving.

Serves 3 to 4 as an entrée, 4 to 6 as an accompaniment.

Major Protein up to 4 servings; *Minor Protein* for more than 4

Variation: Cheese Pie may also be prepared with High Protein Mix (page 190).

HIGH PROTEIN MIX

This has a higher protein value than the other mixes and a more pronounced grain flavor.

3 cups whole wheat flour
¼ cup soy flour
¾ cup wheat germ
1 cup nonfat dry milk powder
2½ tablespoons baking powder
1½ teaspoons salt
1 tablespoon nutritional yeast
½ cup oil

In a large bowl, blender, or processor fitted with a plastic mixing blade, combine the dry ingredients and mix well. Slowly add oil, continually mixing until it is completely absorbed.

Store in a closed container in the refrigerator and mix well before each use.

Makes about 7 cups; 1¾ pounds

QUICK PROTEIN BISCUITS

2½ cups High Protein Mix, spooned into measure
½ cup water

Preheat oven to 425°F.

Add water to mix to form an even dough. Knead gently to combine. Pat into a rectangle 1 inch thick. Cut into eight 2-inch squares.

Bake on a lightly oiled pan for 15 to 20 minutes until golden.

Makes 8 biscuits
Minor Protein

QUICK PROTEIN CRACKER BREAD

A crisp cracker that is a real treat with Camembert, Brie, or a vegetable spread. Stored in a dry, airtight wrapper, Cracker Bread will last several weeks.

2½ cups High Protein Mix, spooned into measure
½ cup water
sesame seeds

Preheat oven to 425°F.

Combine mix with water and knead gently to form a dough. Divide dough into 10 balls and roll each into a 4-inch round, ⅛ inch thick.

Place on an oiled baking sheet. Sprinkle with sesame seeds and press gently to help them stick.

Bake for 10 to 12 minutes until golden. Serve warm or cool.

Makes 10 cracker breads
Minor Protein

QUICK PROTEIN MUFFINS

3¼ cups High Protein Mix, spooned into measure
1 cup water
1 egg, beaten
2 to 4 tablespoons honey

Preheat oven to 400°F.

Combine all ingredients, adding the maximum sweetening for a sweet muffin, and stir gently until completely moistened. Spoon into an oiled muffin tin. Bake for 15 to 20 minutes.

Makes 8 muffins
Minor Protein

CORN MIX

A tasty mixture of corn and wheat.

    2 cups whole wheat flour
    2 cups cornmeal
    1 cup nonfat dry milk powder
    2½ tablespoons baking powder
    1½ teaspoons salt
    ½ cup oil

In a large bowl, blender, or processor fitted with a plastic mixing blade, combine the dry ingredients and mix well. Slowly add oil, continually mixing until it is completely absorbed.

Store in a closed container in the refrigerator and mix well before each use.

Makes about 6½ cups; 1¾ pounds

QUICK CORN BISCUITS

    1¾ cups Corn Mix, spooned into measure
    ¼ cup water

Preheat oven to 425°F.

Combine mix and water, kneading gently to form a dough that holds together. If too dry or crumbly, add a few drops water. Pat into rectangle ½ inch thick and score with a fork into six 2-inch sqaures. Do not break apart.

Place on an oiled baking sheet and bake for 15 to 20 minutes until nicely browned. Break apart to serve.

Makes 6 biscuits
Minor Protein

QUICK CORN CRISPS

A corn–wheat cracker for snacking or traditional cracker use. Stored in a covered tin these will keep a long time.

1¾ cups Corn Mix, spooned into measure
¼ cup water

Preheat oven to 425°F.

Combine mix and water, kneading gently to form a dough that can be rolled. If too dry or crumbly, add additional water.

Roll on a lightly floured surface into a large rectangle that is ⅛ inch thick. (If you find it more comfortable, roll only half at a time.)

Transfer dough to an oiled, floured baking sheet and score with a fork into desired shapes and sizes for breaking apart later.

Bake for 10 minutes, or until golden. Cool on a rack and crack on lines.

Makes ½ pound crackers
Minor Protein

QUICK CORN MUFFINS

2¾ cups Corn Mix, spooned into measure
1 egg, beaten
2 tablespoons molasses or honey
1 cup water

Preheat oven to 400°F.

Place mix in a bowl. Add remaining ingredients and mix gently until completely moistened.

Spoon into an oiled muffin tin, filling two-thirds full for medium muffins, three-fourths for large ones.

Bake for 15 to 20 minutes until lightly browned.

Makes 8 to 10 muffins
Minor Protein

CORN FLATS

A tortilla-like bread that should be served warm, spread with butter if you wish; it goes well with Mexican, Indian, Chinese, or typically American soups, salads, and stews.

1½ cups Corn Mix, spooned into measure
¼ cup water

Stir water into mix to form a soft ball of dough that can be handled. Cover with a cloth and let rest for 15 to 30 minutes.

Divide into 4 balls. Roll each on a lightly floured surface into a thin circle, about 7 inches around.

Heat a griddle, heavy skillet, or use the top of a wood-burning stove. Wipe with an oil-moistened paper towel and, when quite hot, cook rounds one at a time, until each side is flecked with brown. To keep warm and pliable, stack and cover with a cloth. Serve while still hot.

Makes 4 breads; serves 2 to 4

Minor Protein

Note: To make individual flat breads, combine 6 tablespoons mix and 1 tablespoon water.

Desserts

BANANA CREAM

A creamy frozen fruit dessert that is as pleasing to the palate as ice cream, but with much less fat and sugar.

1 ripe banana
1 tablespoon orange juice
1½ tablespoons honey
1 cup ricotta cheese

In a blender or processor puree banana with orange juice and honey. When smooth, add ricotta and process until smooth and light.

Transfer to a 1-pint container and freeze. Serve firm but not quite hard. If frozen solid, let stand at room temperature for about 10 minutes before serving.

Makes 1 pint; serves 4

Minor Protein

Variations: For *Strawberry Cream*, replace banana with 1 cup fresh cut-up berries; 2 tablespoons honey may be needed, depending on the sweetness of the fruit.

For *Peach Cream*, replace banana with 1 cup peeled fresh peach pieces and increase honey to 2 tablespoons. Or, use 1 cup drained peaches canned in unsweetened juice and replace orange juice with 1 tablespoon canning liquid.

BANANA SOFT-SERVE

It takes nothing more than a banana from the freezer to produce one of the creamiest, smoothest-textured frozen desserts around. It's hard to believe there is neither cream nor sweetening in this confection.

Place bananas, 1 per serving, directly in the freezer. They do not need to be peeled, but if you wish to, they must be wrapped airtight for freezing. Otherwise, the skin itself will serve as protection.

Just before serving, remove skin with a small paring knife, cut frozen banana into chunks, and place in a processor fitted with a steel blade or in the blender. Process until banana breaks up, passes the icy stage, and becomes creamy and whipped with air. The consistency will be that of frozen custard. Spoon into a bowl, a paper cup, or a cone, and dig in.

Note: If peeling more than 1 or 2 frozen bananas at a time, protect fingers with gloves or a soft kitchen cloth.

Variations: You can add frozen berries or peaches and whip these with the banana, but for best texture at least half the mixture should be banana.

FROZEN PINEAPPLE

A sugarless ice pop.

cubes or spears of fresh or canned pineapple
lollipop sticks or toothpicks with sharp tip removed

Insert a handle into each piece of pineapple. Wrap in plastic wrap and freeze. Eat frozen off the stick.

PINEAPPLE SHERBET

You can turn canned pineapple into a light, refreshing dessert in minutes with some advance planning. You should allow at least 3 hours to freeze pineapple and can keep the can in the freezer for as long as 3 months.

20-ounce can crushed pineapple in unsweetened juice, frozen in can until solid

Just before serving, remove both ends of the can and break up the frozen mass with a cleaver. Process in the blender or a food processor fitted with a steel blade until fruit is of sherbet consistency, stopping and stirring with a rubber spatula as needed until mixture is smooth. Serve immediately.

Serves 6

Note: A mere 60 calories per serving, this sherbet is not very sweet; although a little honey can be added, it is best unsweetened so that its delicate pineapple flavor can be appreciated. Leftovers can be refrozen and served with or without reprocessing.

FROZEN JUICICLES

Ice cubes are fun to eat even when they have no flavor. These juice cubes are a delightful summer treat. Hold them in paper towels or cups for eating out of hand.

1½ cups juice
1 ice cube tray

Pour juice into an ice cube tray. Freeze for several hours until firm.

Makes 12 cubes

Note: Especially good juice choices include pineapple, orange, and apple–berry blends. Grape is not recommended, as it stains badly if it drips on clothing or furniture.

FROZEN STRAWBERRY YOGURT

2 cups unsweetened frozen strawberries
2 tablespoons orange juice
3 tablespoons honey
1 cup yogurt

Puree berries, orange juice, and honey in a blender or processor fitted with a steel blade. Add yogurt and process quickly until well mixed.

Pour into a shallow 8- or 9-inch metal pan and chill for about 2 hours until firm.

Return to the blender or processor, breaking into chunks. Puree again until smooth. This may require a little stopping and scraping until yogurt begins to soften. When the mixture is as creamy as soft custard, pack it into a 1-pint freezer container and freeze solid. Remove from the freezer for 10 to 15 minutes before serving to soften.

Makes 1 pint; serves 4 to 6
Minor Protein
Note: About 100 calories per serving.

FRUIT JUICE GEL (GELATIN)

Any fruit juice can be used in this manner with the exception of fresh or frozen pineapple which inhibit the gelling action.

1 envelope unflavored gelatin
2 cups juice

Sprinkle gelatin over ½ cup juice in a saucepan. Place over low heat and stir constantly for 3 to 5 minutes until gelatin dissolves. Remove from heat, stir in remaining cold juice, pour into individual dishes or a single mold, and chill until set.

Makes 2 cups; serves 4

Variations: A mixture of juices works quite well; among our favorites: ½ cup apple juice and 1½ cups orange juice; 1 cup canned pineapple juice and 1 cup orange juice; 1 cup grape juice and 1 cup apple or orange juice. Some of the premixed combinations like strawberry–apple and boysenberry–apple are also recommended.

For *Fruited Gel*, chill mixture for 20 to 30 minutes until thickened to the consistency of unbeaten egg whites. Fold in up to 1 cup fresh, frozen, or canned fruit. Chill until set.

FRUIT JUICE GEL (AGAR)

1½ teaspoons granulated agar
2 cups juice

Sprinkle agar over juice in a saucepan. Let stand for a few minutes to soften, then bring to a simmer and cook, stirring to dissolve. Simmer for 5 minutes.

Pour into serving dishes or a single mold. Although thickening will take place at room temperature, chilling is recommended as it speeds the process and gels taste best cold anyway.

Makes 2 cups; serves 4

Variations: Prepare with any juice you wish or make a fruited version as directed above.

TORTONI

This simple yet luxurious Italian dessert is frozen in paper cups.

1 cup ricotta cheese
2 tablespoons honey
½ teaspoon almond extract
4 teaspoons finely ground almonds

Whip ricotta, honey, and almond extract with a rotary or electric beater until light and fluffy. Line a muffin tin with 4 paper liners and fill with mixture. Sprinkle each with 1 teaspoon ground almonds. Freeze. When solid, remove from tin and wrap in freezer bags or foil. Let stand for 10 to 15 minutes at room temperature to soften slightly before serving.

Serves 4
Minor Protein
Note: These are a mere 130 calories each when made with part-skim milk ricotta.

TAHINI CUSTARD

A delicious nondairy pudding that enhances the value of any meal that features beans.

2 cups apple juice
2½ tablespoons honey
2½ tablespoons arrowroot
2 tablespoons water
¼ cup tahini

Combine apple juice and honey and bring to a boil. Make a paste of arrowroot and water. Stir into hot juice and cook over low heat until thick. Stir in tahini and cook until smooth. Pour into a large bowl or 4 individual dishes, cool to room temperature, then chill.

Makes 2 cups; serves 4
Protein Complement

QUICK-COOKING CUSTARD

For custard lovers who won't take the time to bake it just for themselves, this quick top-of-the-stove version is quite acceptable. Although it does not have the fine, smooth texture of the baked, it is nonetheless tender and just as flavorful.

1 egg
¾ cup milk (whole preferred)
2 tablespoons honey or a combination of honey and
    maple syrup or molasses
¼ teaspoon vanilla extract
nutmeg

Beat egg with milk, sweetening, and vanilla, using a fork or wire whisk. Pour into two custard cups. Sprinkle with nutmeg.

Place a wire rack in the bottom of a pot deep enough to hold custard cups when covered. Place filled cups on rack. Add enough hot water to reach about halfway up the cups. Bring water to a boil; cover pot and cook over fairly low heat, keeping water just at a boil for about 15 minutes until custard is set and a knife inserted comes out clean. Transfer to a rack to cool to room temperature, then chill.

Serves 2
Minor Protein

FAVORITE FRUIT SALAD

Almost any combination of fruit can serve you well in fruit salad, but to make the mixture extra special we have two recommendations: walnuts and dates.

> 2 apples, peeled and sliced
> 2 bananas, peeled and diced
> other fruits in season as desired
> juice of 3 oranges
> 8 to 12 dates
> generous amount walnut pieces

Combine apples and bananas with other fruits in season in a bowl. Add orange juice to the fruit to preserve the color and furnish a syrup. Cut dates into small pieces and add to fruit. Top with an impressive amount of nuts.
Serves 4

MARINATED FIGS

Figs are one of the sweetest of fruits; set to marinate in juice, they produce a dessert of elegant simplicity.

> 12 dried golden figs (about ½ pound)
> 2 tablespoons raisins
> 1¼ cups apple juice
> 2 tablespoons lemon juice

Combine figs, raisins, and apple juice in a small saucepan. Bring to a boil and simmer for just 1 minute. Remove from heat, add lemon juice, and set in the refrigerator to chill. Let marinate for at least 8 hours (and preferably a full day) before serving.
Serves 4 to 6

Note: Figs can be cut up in the serving dish before they are presented, or can be served whole with a knife and fork. For more elegant presentation, top figs with a small portion of fine-quality ice cream.

DRIED FRUIT COMPOTE

Stewed dried fruit keeps for weeks in the refrigerator and can be a great asset for a quick dessert or even a breakfast combined with yogurt.

2 cups dried fruit (prunes, raisins, peaches, apricots, figs, and apples in any proportion)
2 cups water
1 cinnamon stick
2 thin slices unpeeled orange
2 thin slices unpeeled lemon

Combine all ingredients in a saucepan and bring to a boil. Cover, remove from heat, and let cool to room temperature. Transfer to storage container and chill several hours before using.

Makes about 1 quart

BUTTERED PEARS

A delicate yet very comforting winter dessert.

    2 tablespoons butter
    1 tablespoon lemon juice
    2 tablespoons honey
    4 medium pears
    nutmeg

Melt butter in a large skillet. Stir in lemon and honey. While butter melts, peel pears and cut lengthwise into eighths, cutting away the pits.

Place pear wedges in hot honey-butter and sauté, turning carefully and cooking until pears are tender but not mushy, about 5 to 8 minutes. Transfer pears with some of the butter sauce to individual serving plates. Sprinkle with nutmeg and serve while still warm.

Serves 4

Variation: Substitute apples for the pears.

STEAMED APPLES

For fewer than 6 servings, steaming rather than baking apples has many advantages: it takes less time, uses less energy, and allows partial cooking in advance with easy reheating just before serving without inconvenience to the cook.

    1 to 5 apples
    ½ to 2½ tablespoons honey or maple syrup
    raisins and nuts (optional)

Wash apples, peel upper third, and remove core. Place bottom-up on steamer and steam for 10 minutes.

Invert and drizzle a little honey or maple syrup over exposed peeled flesh and into hollow. If desired, raisins and nuts can be inserted into the core space. Continue steaming until apples are fork-tender, about 10 minutes for medium apples. Serve warm, garnished, if desired, with a little yogurt, sour cream, plain cream, or ice cream, and a sprinkling of cinnamon, nutmeg, and grated nutmeats.

Serves 1 to 5

Note: If prepared in advance, undercook slightly and warm just before serving by steaming for 2 minutes. Since only 5 apples fit comfortably in the steaming basket at one time, baking is a more efficient method for 6 or more servings.

BROILED ORANGE

Broiling brings out the sweetness of an orange and makes an excellent low-calorie, fat-and-sugar-free dessert. It is especially welcome in winter when cold desserts seem less appealing. However, the heating of citrus fruit on a regular basis is not recommended as it destroys vitamin C.

1 good-size eating orange
¼ teaspoon cinnamon
⅛ teaspoon nutmeg

Cut orange in half crosswise and remove any seeds. Using a serrated grapefruit knife, cut around each section. Sprinkle some cinnamon and nutmeg over each half. Broil for 5 minutes, or until juice begins to bubble and orange is heated throughout. Serve at once.

Serves 2

BANANES AUX PECANES

A Louisiana Creole dessert.

4 bananas
1 cup chopped pecans
⅓ cup molasses
1 tablespoon butter

Peel bananas and slice in half crosswise. Slice each half lengthwise into four pieces (32 slices in all).

Layer half the bananas in a greased 1-quart baking dish. Cover with pecans and top with remaining bananas. Pour molasses over all. Cut butter into bits and arrange on top.

Broil 6 inches from the heat for about 10 minutes, or until bananas begin to brown. Serve warm.

Serves 6

MONKEYS IN A BLANKET

Banana baked in bread is a quick and easy dessert that can be made for one or for a crowd.

1 slice whole grain bread
honey or honey-sweetened preserves
½ banana
½ tablespoon melted butter
cinnamon

Preheat oven or toaster oven to 400°F. Roll bread flat with a rolling pin and trim crust. Spread with a thin layer of honey or preserves. Place banana half on bread and wrap jelly-roll fashion.

Melt butter in a shallow baking dish in preheating oven or toaster oven tray. Allow 1 tablespoon for each whole banana. Roll bread-covered banana in melted butter, sprinkle with cinnamon, and bake for 15 minutes until crust is crisp and banana hot and creamy.

Serves 1

Note: Bananas should be served shortly after baking but can be wrapped in bread and refrigerated for advance preparation.

QUICK FRUIT TARTS

A good spur-of-the-moment dessert.

whole grain bread
softened butter
plums, pears, peaches, nectarines, bananas, or
    strawberries
honey
slivered almonds

Preheat oven or toaster oven to 375°F. Cut bread thin and spread with a layer of butter. Cover with fruit of choice cut in slices. Press into butter. Drizzle with honey and top with some slivered almonds. Bake for about 30 minutes until fruit is tender and bread crisp. Serve warm.

ROAST PINEAPPLE

Use this technique to improve a disappointing pineapple.

1 pineapple
2 tablespoons honey
cinnamon

Quarter pineapple after removing top. Leave meat in each quarter in one piece loosened from the rind. Prick surface liberally with a fork. Drizzle 1½ teaspoons honey over each quarter. Sprinkle liberally with cinnamon. Broil for 5 minutes until hot and bubbly. Cut in slices and serve.

DATE-NUT BREAD PUDDING

This dessert requires no cooking, no added sweetening, and is very rich.

1¾ cups fresh whole grain bread crumbs
¼ cup wheat germ
1 cup chopped dates
½ cup mixed chopped almonds, cashews, and
  sunflower seeds
⅔ cup orange juice or a combination of orange and
  apple juice

Combine bread crumbs, wheat germ, dates, and nuts. Add juice until mixture is moist but not soggy. Line a 9-inch pie pan with waxed paper and press mixture into pan. Cover loosely with waxed paper, foil, or plastic wrap. Chill for several hours.

To serve, lift waxed paper with pudding from pan and slice into thin wedges. Serve with honey-sweetened yogurt or sour cream.

Serves 8
Minor Protein

HALVAH

Commercially, halvah is made by blending sesame butter (tahini) with sugar syrup. We have fortified the mixture a little, but the flavor is still the same.

¼ cup tahini
3 tablespoons honey
⅓ cup wheat germ
¼ cup sunflower seeds, ground into meal (about ⅓ cup)

Combine all ingredients until evenly mixed. Shape into two logs, 1 inch in diameter and 6 inches long. Cover with plastic wrap and store in the refrigerator. Cut pieces as needed.
Makes two 6-inch logs
Minor Protein

SOY WHIPPED CREAM

A nondairy whipped topping with good flavor.

8 ounces tofu
1 teaspoon vanilla extract
1½ tablespoons honey
2 tablespoons oil

Combine tofu, vanilla, and honey in a blender or processor fitted with a plastic blade. Process until smooth. With the machine running, gradually add oil through the feeder cap.
Makes ⅔ cup; serves 4 to 6
Protein Complement

WHIPPED ORANGE–SESAME CREAM

A thick, rich nondairy topping that is delicious on plain cakes.

3 tablespoons orange juice
2 tablespoons honey
¼ cup tahini
⅓ cup light oil (safflower or sunflower)

Gradually beat orange juice and honey into tahini until smooth. Slowly beat in oil, pouring in a steady stream as if you were making mayonnaise, until "cream" is thick. This is most easily done in the blender or processor, adding the oil through the feeder cap. If done by hand, use a wire whisk and have a helper pour in the oil as the whipping takes place.

Makes ⅔ cup
Protein Complement

"SNACKS"

The value of nuts and seeds increases when they are munched ensemble rather than individually on separate occasions. There are many prepackaged "snacks" utilizing this principle; known as "trail mix" and "gorp," they are the best picnic-hiking-lunchbox stuffers around.

The exact proportion of ingredients is not crucial. We prefer a large quantity of sunflower and pumpkin seeds because they are lower in fat than other nuts. The addition of soynuts and/or wheat germ ensures good protein.

▪ As a general guideline, combine several cups of sunflower and pumpkin seeds with about a quarter as much sesame seeds. Add about 1 cup each of almonds, peanuts, unroasted cashews, soynuts, and wheat germ.

- For a sweet mix, add 1 cup of raisins and about the same amount of chopped dates.
- You can also add some shredded unsweetened coconut, carob chips, banana chips, diced dried pineapple, diced dried apple, or dried apricot, peach, and pear halves.
- Keep this mix in airtight containers for a handy snack.

Minor Protein

HOT WET NUTS

A special treat for homemade sundaes.

2 tablespoons butter
½ cup chopped nuts
¼ cup maple syrup
2 tablespoons water

Melt butter in a small skillet and brown nuts lightly over low heat. Stir in maple syrup and water and simmer for 2 minutes.

Makes ⅔ cup; serves 6

Beverages

Many people who, like W. C. Fields, disdain water as a beverage find sparkling water much more to their taste. Both imported and domestic naturally sparkling mineral waters have become very popular. Certainly, they are pleasant, refreshing, noncaloric drinks, but it is unlikely that they possess the curative powers that many attribute to them. Moreover, many are not as naturally "sparkling" as they claim and may have had the carbonation adjusted.

This is not to dissuade you from their use, but to make you aware of their true nature and also to inform you of an alternative that is not so very different from costly mineral waters. The alternative, "seltzer" water, commonly available on tap at soda fountains, is a carbon dioxide-charged water. After several decades of relative obscurity, it is enjoying a commercial rebirth. Seltzer is more highly charged than most natural sparkling waters. It is like club soda in flavor and bubbliness but does not contain any added sodium salts or artificial flavorings.

Excellent homemade soda pop can be prepared using charged water, as in the following recipe. You may even want to start making charged water at home with a seltzer maker and carbon dioxide pellets that are sold for this purpose.

SELTZER FIZZ

The American Wholefoods soda pop; any juice can be turned into a carbonated beverage by mixing it with seltzer.

juice of choice, including apple, orange, pineapple,
   grape, and various fruit blends
seltzer

Fill a glass about two-thirds with juice. Add seltzer until juice is diluted to taste and quite fizzy. Exact proportions vary, depending on the juice as well as your own preferences, but a general ratio of 2 parts juice to 1 part sparkling water is about right.

VEGETABLE COCKTAIL

A blend of tomato juice and fresh vegetables for a "salad in a glass."

1 slice green pepper
1 scallion
½ medium cucumber, peeled
3 sprigs parsley
2 cups tomato juice
1 teaspoon lemon juice
ice

Cut up vegetables and combine in a blender or processor fitted with a steel blade. Add ½ cup tomato juice and blend until smooth. Add remaining juice and lemon juice and blend briefly to combine.

Serve over ice to thin, as this is somewhat thicker than plain juice.

Makes about 3 cups; serves 4

Note: Best consumed soon after preparation; if stored, keep in a covered container and shake well before serving.

LEMONADE

It is just as easy to make real fresh lemonade as it is to reconstitute the frozen concentrate.

3 tablespoons honey
1 cup warm water
½ cup lemon juice (about 2⅓ lemons)
2 cups cold water

Dissolve honey in warm water. Add lemon juice and cold water, and chill.

Makes about 1 quart

Variations: For a delicious *Fruit Punch,* combine lemonade with orange juice, apple juice, cherry apple, grape, and similar sweet fruit juices to taste.

For *Lemon-Limeade,* use ¼ cup lemon juice and ¼ cup lime juice.

CRANBERRY JUICE COCKTAIL

2 cups cranberries
3 cups water
about ⅓ cup honey
1 teaspoon lemon juice

Combine berries and water in a saucepan and simmer for 15 minutes to extract juice. Mash gently with a spoon to aid the process.

Strain juice through a sieve and once again crush berries to release juices without actually pushing the pulp through the strainer.

Add honey and lemon juice while still hot. Stir to melt. Taste and if too tart, adjust honey to taste. Chill.

Makes 1½ pints

Note: Cranberry juice can be either served straight or mixed with apple, orange, or grape juice.

After juice is extracted, about ½ cup pulp will remain. To make *Cranberry Jelly*, add about 1 tablespoon honey to this pulp.

Both the juice and the jelly made with the pulp will keep up to two weeks with refrigeration.

FRESH FRUIT DRINK

A blend of fresh fruit and juice with unlimited possibilities.

1 cup diced fresh fruit of choice (berries, melon,
    nectarines, or peeled peach or plums)
½ cup fruit juice of choice (orange, pineapple,
    apple, or grape)
¼ cup ice

Puree fruit in a blender or processor fitted with a steel blade, adding juice to make puree smooth. Gradually add ice and process until completely dissolved.

Makes 1¼ cups; serves 2

Variation: For a *Fresh Fruit Fizz*, process fruit and juice as described, add ¼ cup carbonated water, and serve over ice.

PARTY PUNCH

No need for canned or dry-mix beverages.

2 cups orange juice
2 cups apple juice
1 cup grape juice
2 cups seltzer or ice

Combine the juices. Just before serving, add seltzer or ice.

Makes 1½ quarts
Variation: For *Virgin Sangria,* add 1 cup sliced seasonal fruit to the juices and let marinate.

JANE'S SCHLURPY

A blender drink with an icy head that makes a hot weather treat.

1½ cups one or a combination of juices (orange, grape, pineapple, apples, or other favorites)
1½ cups ice or 12 ice cubes

Combine juice and ice in a blender and process at high speed until most of the ice is liquefied. Pour into tall glasses. An icy head will rise.

Makes 3 cups (serves 2 generously, 4 more sparingly)

ORANGE JULIA

Like drinking a creamsicle.

1½ cups orange juice
1 teaspoon honey
¼ teaspoon vanilla extract
2 tablespoons nonfat dry milk powder
2 ice cubes

Combine all ingredients in a blender or processor and run at high speed until ice is liquefied. Or, whip with a beater or shake in a jar until ice melts. Serve at once.
Serves 2

THICK SHAKE

Rich enough to eat with a spoon.

½ cup sliced strawberries, banana, peach,
    cantaloupe or other fruit of choice
¾ cup combined apple and orange juice
¼ cup nonfat dry milk powder
4 ice cubes

Puree fruit in a blender or processor fitted with a steel blade.

Add remaining ingredients and whip until ice dissolves and mixture is light and thick. Pour into glasses. Eat with a spoon.
Makes 2 cups; serves 2
Minor Protein
Variation: For a shake you can drink, increase juice to 1 or 1½ cups, or add ½ cup yogurt or milk.

HERB TEA AND CEREAL "COFFEE"

There is a wide variety of herbs that can be used for tea, and as most are caffeine-free, they are often preferred to black-leaf teas and coffee. Herbs are not without their own effects, however. Some, like camomile, are relaxants. Some, like peppermint, are noteworthy for their soothing effect on the digestive system. Both gingseng and maté are potent stimulants. Other herbs act as appetite depressants, laxatives, sedatives, etc. Because they are of plant origin, some may also cause allergic reactions in sensitive individuals.

While it is best to be aware of the potential medicinal properties of the herbs you select for tea, by and large the herbal blends on the market do not adversely affect most people.

The preparation of herb tea is similar to that of regular tea. Because herbs swell considerably in water, a tea strainer is more practical than a teaball when using loose or bulk herbs. Allow a round teaspoonful for each cup of boiling water. This will make one large mug or two small teacups. (When a pot of tea is desired, use 2 tablespoons herbs per quart of water.) About 3 minutes' brewing time is recommended.

To prepare iced herb tea, increase the proportion to 3 tablespoons herbs per quart of boiling water (2 teaspoons per cup) and brew for 5 minutes. Remove herbs and then chill.

Herb teas lack the bitterness of leaf teas and can generally be served without sweetening or with only a bit of honey. If you wish to sweeten iced herb tea, this is best done before chilling. One teaspoon honey per quart of tea should suffice.

The roasted cereal grain blends that are sold as coffee substitutes are more full-bodied than herb teas, have neither the stimulating effect of coffee nor the medicinal properties of herbs, and make quite a satisfying hot or even iced drink.

As not all cereal coffees are the same, you may want to try several to find the one that appeals most. The addition of a little honey imparts a certain mellowness, while sweetening with molasses makes cereal coffees more robust. With the addition of milk, the resulting "coffee" will be suited to children as well as grown-ups.

Planning the Menu

These sample menus are designed to help orient you in preparing wholefood meals and to simplify what is often the cook's greatest dilemma—planning the menu. The menus are not meant to limit your choices, but rather to illustrate some appropriate food combinations. We have provided different choices within the menus so that the meal can reflect your personal taste preferences rather than ours and still be nutritionally and aesthetically balanced.

Short-Order Wholefoods Meals

Guacamole (page 23)
Tortilla Pyramid (page 66) or
Broccoli Tostados (page 67)
Lemon Greens (page 151) or tossed salad
with Light Mexican Tomato Dressing (page 162)

———————

Fluffy Stuffed Baked Potato (page 98)
raw vegetable sticks with Green Dip (page 25) or
Pimiento-Cheese Dip (page 26)
wholegrain breadstuff

———————

Quick Calzone (page 56) or
Individual Bean Pizza (page 57)
Avocado Cocktail (page 156) or
Marinated Zucchini Sticks (page 38)

Quick, Creamy Onion Pie (page 111) or
Baked Rice and Blue Cheese (page 116)
Carrots with Sunflower Seeds (page 129) or
Baked Asparagus (page 124)
tossed salad with beans
and Bottom-of-the-Bowl Dressing (page 159)

Chef Special Salad (page 47)
salad dressing of choice
Wheat Germ Muffins (page 175) or
Quick Protein Muffins (page 191)

Main Dish Stir-Fry (page 92) over brown rice
or brown rice crackers
chopped fresh cabbage with
Creamy Tofu Garlic Dressing (page 164)
Bread & Spread (page 40)
Herb Tea (page 219)

Creamed Corn Soup (page 14) or
Quick Tomato-Onion Soup (page 18)
Kidney Bean Luncheon Salad (page 44) or
Chopped Bean Liver (page 49) or
Tofu "Chicken" Salad (page 47) sandwich

B.O.B. (page 102) or Sloppy Beans (page 101)
Basic Biscuits (page 174) or whole grain toast
tossed salad with dressing of choice

Instant Soup (page 12) or
Quick Mixed Vegetable Soup (page 17)
Cottage Cheese Cutlets (page 73) or
Rice Pancakes (page 72)
Butter-Steamed Brussels Sprouts (page 126) or
Stir-Fried Green Beans with Garlic (page 131)
or Crispy Fried Beets (page 125)

Mushrooms in Garlic Butter (page 133)
Vegetables Mozzarella (page 93)
whole wheat pasta
mixed greens with Herb Dressing (page 160)

———————

Bean Burgers (page 104) or Soyburgers (page 105)
or Tempeh Burgers (page 63)
Touch-of-Honey Catsup (page 168)
Corn on the Cob (page 130) or
American-Style Potato Salad (page 153)
Greek Coleslaw (page 150) or
salad with Revisionist Dressing (page 161)

———————

One-Pot Baked Macaroni and Cheese (page 79) or
Creamy Pasta with Cheese (page 85)
Italian Sautéed Cucumbers (page 130) or
Steamed Greens (page 132)
Soy Biscuits (page 175)

———————

Tofu with Onions and Cheese (page 113) or
Chick-Peas with Gravy (page 144) or
Spinach and Chick-Peas with Feta (page 103)
Brown "Rice-a-Roni" (page 148) or
Cracked Wheat Pilaf (page 147)
salad with Rich Parsley Dressing (page 160)
Whole Wheat Muffins (page 176)

———————

Mozzarella-Stuffed Tomatoes (page 32) or
Cheese-Stuffed Mushrooms (page 30) or
Oil-Cured Mozzarella
Cold Pasta and Broccoli (page 122)
Quick Bread Sticks (page 188)

———————

Very Quick Curried Chick-Peas (page 145)
Cold Eggplant and Yogurt (page 158)
Butter Nut Grains (page 148) or
brown rice Chapati (page 178) or
Corn Flats (page 194)

———————

Italian Spaghetti Stew (page 83) or
Tomato Shells (page 82)
Garlic-Sesame Bread (page 40)
salad with Italian Dressing (page 160)

Boston Roast (page 106) or
Peanut Butter Loaf (page 107)
Stir-Steamed Vegetables (page 140) or
Hot Dressed Vegetables (page 142)
Ricotta-Cucumber Salad (page 152) or
Yogurt-Cucumber Salad (page 152) or
Carrot-Peanut Salad (page 158)

White Gazpacho (page 21) or
Moroccan Yogurt Soup (page 22)
Hummus (page 24) or
Olive-Bean Salad (page 50)
whole wheat pita or
Quick Light Biscuits (page 186)
Greek Olives (page 36)

Sesame-Bean Pâté (page 50) or
Tomato-Pâté (page 51)
Macaroni Salad (page 154) or
French Pasta Salad (page 154)
Quick Pickles (page 35)
Whole grain bread or crackers or
Quick Protein Cracker Bread (page 191)

The Short-Order Pantry

Many who like the idea of wholefoods cuisine are not that interested in doing much cooking. However, eating does have its own imperatives, and whether you are tired, sick, short of time, or only minimally interested in the kitchen arts, you need ample and nourishing food. This is where the pantry again shows its worth. We offer here a list of long-lasting, well-accepted foods that can provide the basis of a no-cook meal, help to round out a meal you bring in, or serve you when you do want to cook.

Bread and Grains
Brown rice (regular or quick-cooking)
Canned brown bread
Cracked wheat (cooks in 15 minutes)
Hot whole grain cereal of choice
Popping corn
Tacos
Tortillas (frozen)
Wheat germ (refrigerate)
Whole grain breadstuffs (fresh or frozen)
Whole grain cold cereal of choice
Whole grain crackers
Whole grain pasta (cooks in 10 minutes)
Whole wheat pretzels

Nuts, Seeds, Beans
Canned beans
Nuts, seeds, "soynuts" (better than chips with a sandwich)
Peanut butter

Soy milk (packaged for room temperature storage)
Tahini
Tempeh (frozen)
Tofu (fresh or frozen)
Unshelled nuts

Cheese and Dairy
Butter
Cottage, pot, or ricotta cheese
Eggs (some hard-cooked)
Hard-grating cheese like Parmesan
Natural slicing cheeses
Nonfat dry milk powder
Yogurt

Fruits and Vegetables
Canned tomatoes
Dried fruit
Fresh fruit (especially apples, oranges, and lemons, which
    keep longest)
Fresh vegetables (especially onions, celery, carrots, and a
    few potatoes)
Frozen vegetables (unseasoned)
Fruit butter
Fruit canned in juice or water
Honey-sweetened or fruit-juice sweetened preserves
Tomato paste
Tomato sauce

Condiments
Basic seasonings like fresh garlic (stick in the freezer), cin-
    namon, nutmeg, peppercorns, cayenne, oregano, basil,
    dry mustard, paprika, curry powder, chili powder
Canned chilies
Capers
Catsup
Dehydrated soup vegetables
Dried Chinese vegetables
Eggplant caponata

Condiments (cont.)

Honey
Hot pepper sauce
Maple syrup
Mayonnaise
Molasses
Mustard
Oil
Olives
Pickled peppers
Pimientos
Soy sauce
Stuffed grape leaves
Unflavored gelatin or agar
Unsweetened shredded coconut (refrigerate)
Vanilla extract
Vinegar

Beverages

Bottled water
Cereal grain beverage
Coffee
Fruit and vegetable juices
Leaf and herb teas
Seltzer

Other recommended convenience wholefoods (pre-made foods free of chemical additives, coloring, artificial flavor, left in the whole, unrefined state or processed as little as possible), include:

Buckwheat or whole wheat pancake mix
Canned soup
Falafel or burger mix
Salad dressing
Whole grain baking mix

Cooking Basics

Basic Vegetable Cookery

Unless recipe directions give other recommendations,
here is general advice for preparing vegetables.

Artichoke, Globe: Remove small leaves at base. Cut
top half off each leaf with a kitchen scissors. Trim end of
stem, but leave stem intact unless artichoke is to be stuffed,
in which case stem should be removed so artichoke will
stand upright. To remove choke for stuffing artichoke, spread
leaves, cut away the small, light leaves in the middle, and
scrape off all the hairy center with a small paring knife.
When trimming is completed, rinse under cold water. If
artichoke will not be cooked immediately, place in a bath
of cold water to which the juice of a lemon or 1 heaping
tablespoon flour has been added. This will prevent discol-
oration of the leaves. When ready to cook rinse again. If
recipe requires artichokes to be cut, do so one by one as
they are added to the pot.

Artichokes, Jerusalem: Scrub with vegetable brush
under cold running water. Peel to use raw or in a casserole
or stew. Otherwise cook first, then peel; the skin is not
good to eat.

Asparagus: Wash in cold water. Trim stem where it
snaps easily when bent. If desired, save the ends for vegetable stock.

Avocado: Prepare as close to serving time as possible.
Cut from tip to tip to remove wedges, loosening gently

from the pit. To forestall browning, keep pit in contact with unused portion. To use the entire fruit at once, cut in half from tip to tip and twist gently to loosen from pit. Remove skin with a small paring knife; sometimes you will find you can even peel the meat off the skin without a knife, or scoop it out with a spoon. Douse with lemon juice to maintain color.

Beans (green or yellow wax): Wash by sloshing around in basin full of cold water, rubbing to remove any dirt. Then rinse by handfuls under cold running water and drain in colander or salad spinner. Trim ends by snapping. If shorter pieces are desired, section by snapping as well.

Beans (pod): Beans still in the pod should be washed in cold water and cooked either in the shell (the beans will then slip right out) or shelled as for fresh peas.

Beets: Remove tops without cutting into bulb. Scrub surface gently with a vegetable brush under cold water. Peel tough skin before shredding or slicing. To cook whole, leave peel intact and remove after cooking to minimize the beet color bleeding.

Beet Greens: See Greens.

Broccoli: Wash in cold running water. If buds are very compact and you suspect the presence of insects, soak up to 15 minutes in a saltwater or a vinegar-water bath. Rinse under cold water and cut as recipe indicates. If stalks seem thick or fibrous, peel with a paring knife or a vegetable peeler to reveal the inner light green core, which is very sweet and tender. Cut a slit up the stem of wide stalks to shorten cooking time to match that of the quicker-cooking buds.

Brussels Sprouts: Wash under cold running water. Trim tough or discolored stem ends.

Cabbage: For salads or general cooking, cut heads in half through the core and rinse under cold water. If cabbage appears to be buggy, soak up to 15 minutes in saltwater or a vinegar-water bath. Rinse in plain water before use.

To prepare cabbage leaves for stuffing, remove core with a small paring knife and loosen any leaves that easily separate from the head. For leaves that are difficult to separate, heat enough water in a large pot to cover the cabbage, then plunge into boiling water, cover and cook for three minutes. Remove and rinse immediately in cold running water until cool enough to handle. Gently peel off as many leaves as you can remove easily. When this becomes difficult, plunge cabbage back into boiling water and repeat the process. As the outer leaves are removed, you may have to cut around the stem end again to disconnect leaves. The entire head should be easy to separate leaf by leaf using this method.

For stuffing, each leaf must be pliable enough to roll without cracking the rib. Any leaves that are not flexible should be placed back in boiling water briefly until they can be bent.

Carrots: Wash under cold running water and scrub with a vegetable brush. Peel only if the skin is thick or there are places where dirt cannot be scrubbed free. If desired, save peelings for stock. Trim off any green areas at stem end.

Cauliflower: Remove tough outer leaves; small, tender leaves can be reserved for the soup pot. Soak whole head in saltwater or vinegar-water for up to 15 minutes to drive out insects. If the vegetable is to be divided into "florets," break apart or cut with a small paring knife before washing, then simply rinse under cold water or soak if it appears necessary. The core is quite tasty and can be sliced raw into salads or cooked along with the buds.

Celery: Wash each stalk individually under cold running water, paying particular attention to the dirt at the base. Trim sparingly at the base and reserve, if desired, for soup or stock. If leaves are not to be used, save for soup.

Chard: See Greens.

Chicory: See Greens.

Chinese Cabbage: The center leaves of this elongated, green leafy vegetable are usually dirt-free; only the cleaning of the outer portions need concern you if the entire head is cut up at once, rather than divided leaf by leaf. Run under cold water and rub gently with hands to clean.

Collards: See *Greens.*

Corn: Don't do anything until just before cooking. Then remove the husk and silk and rinse under cold water only if necessary to remove the silky strands. Corn may be cooked whole, cut into sections still on the cob, or the kernels may be cut away from the cob before cooking. To remove kernels, cut as close to the cob as you can. If you cut in the kernels, you will lose some of the sweet milk. Any of the cob still attached to the kernels can be pulled off with your hands, but it won't hurt you to eat it.

Cucumbers: If cucumber is waxed, as most of those sold commercially are, peel as sparingly as possible before use. Unwaxed cucumbers just need a good rinsing. Seeds need not be removed, but if you are shredding the cucumber and object to the seeds, cut lengthwise and scrape seeds free with the tines of a fork.

Eggplant: Wash under cold running water. Peel with a paring knife or vegetable peeler only if directed.

To char skins for peeling, secure whole eggplant on a skewer, long-handled fork, or a thin, sturdy green branch and hold over a flame, rotating until well blackened on all sides and meat is soft. Remove from heat and, when cool enough to handle, pull peel off by hand. Any pieces that cling can be trimmed with a paring knife.

To bake for peeling, place in a 350° to 375°F. oven in an unoiled pan and bake until quite tender, 30 to 45 minutes, depending on size. When cool enough to handle, remove skin as with charred eggplant.

Salting the eggplant to "extract the bitter juices" is not recommended, although you may encounter a recipe or two here where the eggplant is salted first to soften it for rolling.

Endive: See *Greens.*

Greens (including all lettuce, wild greens, spinach, chard, herbs, etc.): Slosh about in a basin of cold water to loosen dirt. Wash handfuls under cold running water and drain in a salad spinner or colander. Repeat process if any dirt remains. You may sometimes have to rub leaves with your hands to dislodge soil. To dry greens, pat with a towel or give them a whirl in a salad spinner. Or, put them in a mesh basket, take it outside, and swing basket quickly with a circular motion to shake off moisture.

Horseradish: Because it is not readily available, you will not find this vegetable included in our recipes. However, if you wish to use it, peeling is advised although it is best left until the last minute to prevent browning.

Jicama: As you might expect from its appearance, the skin is not edible. Remove with a peeler or paring knife, then rinse the portion you are going to use.

Kale: See *Greens.*

Leeks: These can be extremely sandy inside. The best way to get to the sand is to make a long lengthwise slit penetrating just to the center. Then rinse under cold running water, using your fingers to expose the inner surfaces to the water to flush out the sand. Cut away the roots and the dry part of the green end; use all the light portions and the fresh-looking green tops.

Mushrooms: For us the most tedious kitchen job is the cleaning of mushrooms. Mushrooms should never be soaked, as this makes them spongy, and it is best to expose them to water as briefly as possible during cleaning. The preferred method of cleaning is to rub them with a damp paper towel or a soft brush. Peeling is only needed when they are quite discolored or old. No trimming is needed unless the base of the stem is encrusted with dirt or badly damaged.

Okra: Wash under cold running water, rubbing with your hands to dislodge any dirt. Pods can be cooked whole, but if they are cut, discard the stem portion.

Onions: Remove papery outer layers only. Washing is unnecessary. Chill before cutting to reduce tears.

Parsnips: Scrub with a vegetable brush to remove dirt. Although the skins are bitter, and therefore not recommended for eating, it is best to cook them with the skins on whenever possible and then peel with the tip of a paring knife.

Peas: Wash before shelling and shell just before use. Edible pod peas, which do not need shelling, generally require trimming at the ends with a small paring knife.

Peppers, Hot: Hot peppers are prepared in the same manner as sweet ones, but you must be extremely careful, for many are as hot to the touch as they are to the taste. If you are sensitive, wear rubber gloves when you cut them, particularly if the seeds are exposed. (Thin surgical-type gloves are useful.) Roasting and peeling enhance flavor but are not mandatory.

Peppers, Sweet: Rinse in cold water. Cut and remove seeds and any thick white membranes. When blanching is called for (to shorten cooking), steam, or plunge into boiling water for the time specified. When roasting is called for (to remove the skin), hold on a long-handled fork or skewer and rotate over a flame until the skin blisters. When cool enough to handle, rub skin off with fingers. Any difficult spots can be removed with a paring knife. To roast several at a time, char the skins under a broiler.

Plantains: To prevent browning, peel just before cooking as you would a banana. If cooking is delayed, soak in salted water; pat dry before using.

Potatoes: Scrub well with a vegetable brush under cold running water. Do not soak. Cut away any eyes and green portions. Peel only if it is specifically indicated in the recipe or if the skins are very thick or impossible to wash clean. Potatoes discolor rapidly on exposure to air, so, when possible, cut them just before use. Otherwise browning can be reduced by soaking them in cold water, although this is not a nutritionally sound method. A slightly less effective but more wholesome approach would be to keep them in a covered container in the refrigerator.

Pumpkin: The peel is not edible but is best removed after cooking, when practical. If unpeeled, wash before cooking.

Radish: Wash and scrub gently with a vegetable brush or rub with fingers.

Rutabaga: See Turnips.

Scallion: Rinse under cold running water to clean, and dry. Trim off the root and unsightly portions at the top. Use both green and white parts unless otherwise instructed.

Shallots: Remove outer papery layers. No need to wash.

Spinach: See Greens.

Squash (hard rind): Yellow- and orange-fleshed varieties, as well as patty pan and spaghetti squash, have inedible peels. Once again, it is best to cook these with the peel on and either eat the meat directly from the "shell" or cut it free before use. For stews and soups, however, peeling prior to cooking is necessary; this may be easier to do with a small, sharp paring knife than a vegetable peeler, depending on how thick the rind is and how skilled you are. Try to keep the trimming minimal.

Squash (soft rind): Zucchini and yellow crookneck varieties, with soft, edible rinds, need only rinsing under cold water prior to use. Salting is not recommended except in those recipes where salt is used to extract the moisture from the shredded vegetable for use in salads (when the water content would cause thinning of other ingredients.)

Sweet Potatoes and Yams: These potato skins are generally tough. When the vegetable is cooked whole, peel can be removed after cooking if desired.

Tomatoes: Although we do not peel tomatoes for most uses, for canning and some sauces it is best to do so. Charring the skin by holding the tomato on a skewer or long-handled fork over an open flame imparts an outdoorsy flavor as it loosens the skin, but if you have many to peel, this may be too time-consuming a method. In volume, it is easiest to plunge them into a pot of boiling water for a minute until the skins crack, then cool them quickly under cold running water; when they are cool enough to handle, the skin will slip off easily with the help of a fingernail or small paring knife.

Turnips and Rutabagas: These vegetables belong to the same family and are treated similarly. Generally, they are waxed prior to commercial sale. If so, peel them first, whether they are to be used raw or cooked. If they are not waxed, the skin of turnips can be eaten; however, rutabaga skin is too thick and tough to be enjoyable, and so should be removed either before or after cooking.

Basic Bean Cookery

Beans are an important staple in the wholefoods kitchen; the dried form offers the widest variety, best flavor, and greatest economy. Although canned beans are handy as a backup, they do not compare with the home-cooked kind.

So Much Food, So Little Effort

Although beans seem to take a long time to prepare, they require very little of the cook. All varieties are handled in a similar manner and we have included the most common methods of preparation plus a newer, convenient "freezer method" for those with a tight schedule or a small household.

With the exception of split peas, lentils, limas, and special "no soak" brands, dried beans should be pre-soaked to reduce cooking time. There are two standard pre-soaking techniques.

Regular soak: Rinse beans in cool water and drain them. Place in a large pot with two or three times their volume of water and let stand for about eight hours. This effortless task can take place overnight or while you are out during the day. If soaking time will be more than 12 hours, refrigerate beans during soaking to prevent fermentation.

Quick soak: Place the rinsed, drained beans in a pot with two to three times their volume of water. Bring to a boil, simmer for two minutes, cover, remove from heat, and let stand for one to two hours.

Note: Be sure to allow room for expansion in the pot, since dried beans will about triple in volume during cooking.

Cooking is the same after either soaking method; bring the pot of beans and the soak water to a boil, cover, and simmer, keeping heat as low as possible until tender. Use the timetable that follows as a guide. Some research has shown that if you drain off the soak water before cooking and replace it with fresh, some of the indigestible carbohydrates (ogliosaccharides) that give beans the reputation of being "gassy" will be eliminated. We believe the soak water should be used in cooking because it also contains some water-soluble B vitamins and minerals. If, however, you have trouble digesting beans you may want to try freshwater cooking and compare the results.

For split peas, lentils, limas, and other beans that do not require soaking, just add two to three times their volume of water and cook as for soaked beans.

Low heat will conserve the liquid and also keep beans from splitting, but you should check the water level occasionally and replenish if beans begin to cook dry.

Harmless foam may form on the surface of cooking beans; to reduce it, add a tablespoon of oil.

For flavor, chopped onion, garlic, herbs, fresh chilies, or crushed hot red pepper can be added at any point. Salt and acid ingredients such as tomatoes, lemon juice, vinegar, and wine tend to toughen the outer skin, slowing the cooking process; these flavoring agents should not be added until the beans are almost tender. When salting, add ½ teaspoon salt per cup of dried beans.

Warning: Many cookbooks, particularly older ones, add baking soda to the bean pot; this should be avoided, as the soda destroys the B vitamin thiamine.

Test for Tenderness

One way to test tenderness is to place a few beans on a spoon and blow on them. If they are done, the skin will split. A better way, of course, is to take a few from the pot and taste them. If you plan to use the beans for salads, or as part of a recipe that requires additional cooking, or for storage in the refrigerator or freezer, cook until they are tender but still hold their shape. If you want to puree them for dips and soups, you may want to cook them a little softer. Note that soybeans and chick-peas remain firm-textured even after lengthy cooking.

TIMETABLE AND YIELD FOR COOKING DRIED BEANS

Black beans	1½–2 hours
Black-eyed peas	1½ hours
Fava beans	2–3 hours
Garbanzo beans (chick-peas)	2–3 hours
Kidney beans	1½–2 hours
Lentils	45 minutes
Lima beans	45 minutes–1½ hours
Navy and pea beans	1–1½ hours
Pinto beans	1½–2 hours
Small pink beans	1–1½ hours
Soybeans	3–3½ hours
Split peas	45 minutes
White beans (cannellini)	1½–2 hours

The fresher the beans, the faster they will cook.

Yield: Most dried beans measure 1 to 1⅓ cups per 8 ounces and yield 3 to 3¼ cups cooked beans.

Pressure Cooking

Dried beans may be pressure-cooked, further reducing the cooking time. The tendency of the skins of the beans to clog the steam-release valve can be minimized by oiling the inside of the lid and only filling the vessel half full with water and beans.

The Freezer Method of Bean Cookery

If you are determined to cut cooking time, there is another method you will appreciate. This technique not only saves time but is excellent for those who wish to cook only a small quantity of beans. It is called the Freezer Method and is accomplished as follows.

Pre-soak beans as previously directed. Drain, pat dry, and place *in a single layer* in a shallow pan. Freeze for a few hours until hard, then transfer to airtight freezer bags and return to the freezer for storage. When you need beans in a hurry, dump the frozen beans out of the bag into a pot with boiling water to cover. Most varieties will be done in 30 minutes, and even long-cooking beans like soybeans and chick-peas will be ready to eat within 45 minutes. As most of the expansion of beans takes place during soaking, your cooked yield will be only slightly larger than the volume of frozen beans you begin with.

Substituting Canned Beans

Probably the fastest way to get cooked beans is to have someone else do the job. This is what you are doing when you buy canned beans. While these beans are satisfactory for many recipes, there are drawbacks to their use.

1. Canned beans are almost always highly salted. When using these beans, omit the salt in any recipe. Also, avoid those canned with sugar, MSG, hydrolyzed vegetable protein, modified food starch, and EDTA (a chelating agent that traps minerals).

2. The combined effects of processing and cooking make canned beans softer than home-cooked varieties, almost to the point of mushiness. This will affect the texture of the final dish. Certainly purees are easily achieved with canned

beans, but while some people find they make other dishes smoother and more palatable, many equate them with baby food. Remember, a cooked dish made with canned beans should only be heated long enough to cook the other ingredients and warm the beans themselves.

Ground Beans (Chopped Beat)

Ground beans are the basis of many economical and imaginative recipes. We have come to call beans in this state "chopped beat" as they are similar to ground meat in terms of versatility and use. Chopped beat can be prepared from cooked beans in minutes; the only requirement is that you have one of the following grinding implements.

- The most basic tools for grinding cooked beans are a small hand (Mouli-type) grater and a food mill. The hand grater works best for small amounts; if you are grinding more than four to six servings, the larger food mill is more practical.
- The quickest way to make chopped beat is with either a meat grinder or a food processor, using the steel blade.
- In some recipes ground beans can be replaced with mashed beans—the result of muscle power applied to soft, cooked beans.

Note: The blender is not a suitable tool for grinding beans; in order to process them, the machine requires liquid and thus you end up with a soft puree rather the desired coarse pulp.

Cooked beans must be drained thoroughly before grinding. When the liquid surrounding them has thickened or congealed (as it may upon storage and often does in canned beans), they should be rinsed through a strainer or colander to remove this adherent "gravy." Pat dry with a cloth or paper towel before grinding.

The ideal texture for chopped beat is dry and crumbly. For more textured dishes, you may allow a few pieces of bean to remain. Canned beans and beans that have been cooked soft, once ground, may require additional binding ingredients (flour, bread crumbs, etc.) in order to be shaped according to recipe directions. This is something you will have to judge by feel.

It is preferable to grind beans for use as needed; however, most ground bean recipes can be prepared in advance and kept in the refrigerator or freezer prior to cooking.

Cooking with Tofu

Although tofu is new to many westerners, there is nothing complicated about cooking with it.

During storage, tofu is kept submerged in water and must be drained before use. Unless otherwise directed, remove from the storage container and blot dry with paper towels.

Freezing Tofu

Another aspect of tofu's versatility is that it can be frozen for long-term preservation and to change its texture. This process affects the structure to such an extent that frozen tofu is like an entirely different ingredient. Where the fresh variety is dense and tender, frozen tofu is chewy, with an open, coarse texture; it is much like veal or chicken, making it more familiar and welcome. Freezing also increases its spongelike ability to absorb the flavors of the cooking medium.

To freeze, slice tofu cakes so they are about ½ inch thick. If using small 4-ounce cakes (about 2½ × 2½ × 1 inches), slice in half; slice thicker 8- to 10-ounce blocks in fourths. Wrap each piece of tofu in plastic wrapping. This individual packaging will allow removal of pieces as desired. Make a single moisture-proof package of all the tofu, wrapping it in foil or heavy plastic bags. Freeze as you would any food.

For best eating, use frozen tofu within six months.

Reconstituting Frozen Tofu

Frozen tofu must be defrosted before use, and the recommended procedure is quite different from that used with any other frozen food.

Remove all freezer packaging and place tofu in a deep bowl. Cover with boiling water. Let stand about 10 minutes and drain. If tofu is still partially frozen, repeat the procedure. When completely thawed, rinse with cool water, then press firmly between your palms to expel all moisture and make it as dry as possible. It is now ready to use.

Basic Grain Cookery

Grains are a mainstay of wholefoods meals; they may be served alone or used as an ingredient in the preparation of more complicated recipes. While similar principles control the cooking of all grains, each has its peculiarities as well.

Grains owe their palatability to the interaction between heat and their starchy kernels. Surrounded by steam or boiling liquid, the grain swells and absorbs moisture. The preferred manner of cooking is to provide only as much liquid as the grain can hold, so that it does not need to be drained. Two parts liquid to one part grain is the standard proportion, although when grains are cooked for cereal or pudding the liquid may be increased to three or four times their volume. Cooking may be done in water, broth, juice, or milk.

Boiling water method: Adding the grains to boiling liquid is said to cause them to swell rapidly, with the effect that when cooking has ended, each grain remains separate. To use this method, sprinkle the grain slowly into the boiling liquid, cover the pot, lower the heat so the liquid barely simmers, and cook until the grain is tender and the liquid absorbed.

Cold water method: Other cooks insist that the Oriental method of preparation is superior. Here the grain is rinsed through a sieve under cold water to remove surface starch, transferred to the cooking vessel, covered with cold water that extends one inch above the grain level (this may be slightly less than twice the grain volume), then brought to a boil, covered, and simmered as in the previous method. To trap the steam around the grain as it cooks, the pot must have a tight-fitting cover.

Regardless of the initial approach, during the cooking process the liquid should barely simmer. Furious boiling will cause the grains to burst.

Do not stir while cooking, unless otherwise directed. Stirring loosens the starch from the outer surface and makes grains gummy.

For most savory dishes, salt is added and, although the amount will vary with personal taste, ½ teaspoon salt per cup of dry grain is a sensible guideline. If the cooking medium is highly seasoned, or if additional flavorings will be added to the grain later on, salt may be omitted. (The addition of salt makes rice and millet firmer, adding to their cooking time. You may wish to allow these grains to cook for 15 minutes before salting them.)

When cooking time is almost over, insert a chopstick or poke with a fork to see if all the liquid has been absorbed at the bottom of the pot. Chew a few top grains to check tenderness. If not done, continue to cook, adding a little liquid, if needed, to prevent scorching. If grains are quite tender but a little liquid still remains, uncover partially and cook until dry. When cooking is completed, remove from heat and, if possible, let stand, covered, for 15 minutes before serving. This allows the grains to "set."

Dry-Roasted Grains

Dry roasting refers to the light toasting of uncooked grains without added fat. This makes them both firmer and fluffier and imparts a nutlike flavor. With most grains this is a matter of taste. With buckwheat groats, however, which are generally mixed with beaten egg and dry-roasted before boiling, the result is so superior that they are almost always cooked this way.

To dry-roast, put grains in an unheated, ungreased pot over medium heat. Stir continuously for three to five minutes. You will notice a pleasant aroma and soon a deepening of color in the grains. Do not let them become dark, or the flavor will be burned, not nutty. Add liquid and cook as usual.

Sautéed Grains

Prior to boiling, grains may be sautéed in about 1 tablespoon oil or butter per cup of dry grain. This adds a certain savoriness and often serves as a vehicle for adding other seasonings, including garlic, onion, and small amounts of chopped vegetables. Sautéeing is generally reserved for grain dishes that stand on their own during a meal, not for grains that will later be combined with other foods. Once again, stir continuously while sautéeing until grains are golden, then add liquid and cook as usual.

TIMETABLE AND YIELD
FOR COOKING GRAINS

These figures are approximate and will vary with the volume of grain, the size of the flame, and the fit of the lid.

Brown rice	50 minutes
Cracked wheat (bulgur)	15–20 minutes
Buckwheat groats (kasha)	20 minutes
Millet	30 minutes
Barley	60 minutes
Oats	10 minutes
Couscous	5–10 minutes

Yield: One cup dry grain will produce about three times this amount cooked, or enough for four to six servings, depending on use.

Greater Grains

If you wish to enhance the food value of grains, you can add 1 tablespoon nutritional yeast, or 2 tablespoons wheat germ per cup of dry grain at the end of cooking. Incorporate with a fork, using a light "fluffing" motion.

Helpful Habits

After spending some time in the kitchen, most people develop habits and pick up tricks that keep them organized and help to make the job quicker, easier, and more rewarding.

Good form makes the difference between having a pleasurable, relaxed time in the kitchen and dashing about madly, using twice the number of utensils necessary or being caught without an ingredient in the middle of a recipe. Cooking habits and shortcuts almost always evolve with experience, but a little bit of advice beforehand can quicken the process and help make you feel comfortable from the first.

You will find this Master Rule the key to minimizing disappointment and failure.

MASTER RULE

Begin each recipe by reading it through completely. Gather all the ingredients and appropriate utensils at your work space and prepare pans and oven if necessary. *Do as much measuring, peeling, chopping, etc., as practical before combining ingredients.* You are now ready to assemble, mix, cook, and concentrate on any unfamiliar techniques—mastering the recipe.

Stock the Pantry

Keep your pantry stocked with a variety of the wholefoods you use. See "The Short-Order Pantry" for details.

Have a Repertoire

Cultivate some standard family favorites and some special recipes for entertaining. Even professional chefs have a limited number of specialties, which they add to gradually. The list need not be extensive, but it should be made up of dishes you feel at ease with and ones that can be made from ingredients that are generally on hand.

The Bean Pot and Grain Store

To replace the meat in the freezer you might customarily rely on for a meal, some precooked staples should be built in to your meal planning. Having cooked beans and/or grains on hand provides many options for a quickly prepared meal. Thus, when we make beans, we always cook more than we need for that day. The same goes for rice, cracked wheat, kasha, and other favorite grains. All of these will keep well for about a week in the refrigerator. Even if you don't have a particular recipe in mind, cook up a big pot of beans and/or grains when you are home for a couple of hours or while you are preparing another meal. You can decide what to do with them later. Remember, beans can be frozen if you tire of them before you finish the potful.

Frozen Tofu

With tofu in your freezer at all times, you will have the fixings of many fast meals. One of tofu's more amazing qualities is the wonderful textural changes that occur during freezing. Ordinarily very soft, tofu becomes chewy, more resilient, and quite absorbent after freezing, closer in character to many common protein foods, such as chicken, turkey, fish, and veal. Defrosting takes only about 10 minutes (see "Cooking with Tofu," page 239).

We recommend trying frozen tofu in any recipe in which you find fresh tofu too soft. Experiment with your favorite recipes by replacing protein foods, like those mentioned above, with tofu.

Pre-Made Ingredients

Save steps by anticipating future needs. Foods that you use frequently in grated or chopped form can often be prepared more efficiently in quantity if you have a blender or food processor. Grated cheese, nuts, and fresh bread crumbs keep for a week if refrigerated, and for months if frozen. They can be used directly from the freezer without defrosting. Onions, green pepper, carrots, and celery, which you might otherwise find yourself chopping daily for soups and stews, can be prepared en masse and stored in plastic bags in the freezer for a few weeks with no special processing. However, these are mainly suitable for cooked dishes, where they serve as flavoring agents and are not important for texture.

Flavoring Cubes

We have found cooks are enthusiastic about this time- and work-saving device that we have developed, storing certain flavoring aids as ice cubes. When we open a can of tomato paste, for example, and use only a bit, the rest gets transferred to a designated ice cube tray where it is frozen into two-tablespoon portions. Later, when we need a little tomato paste for seasoning a soup or a salad dressing or for enriching a sauce, we simply drop in a cube or two. In addition, small amounts of leftover soup and vegetable purees and sauces, which appear to be of no use in themselves, make excellent flavoring cubes that can be added to a pot of cooking pasta or grains, a bean or vegetable stew, a soup or sauce, or almost any other dish in need of a little change.

TOMATO CUBES

Frequent reference is made in this book to Tomato Cubes, one of our favorite flavoring aids made from the fine-tasting fresh tomatoes that abound in summer. Tomato cubes are made by cutting up fresh tomatoes and simmering them in a covered pot for 10 to 15 minutes, just until they are soft enough to puree. Press through a food mill or strainer, discard skins, and spoon the pulp into ice cube trays. Place directly in the freezer until solid. Once frozen, transfer the cubes to freezer bags, close tightly, and return to cold storage.

Throughout the winter, when a gravy, soup, or stew needs a lift, we just drop in a couple of cubes. Two cubes can replace ¼ cup tomato juice or one diced fresh tomato in a recipe.

Pre-Washed Salad

Although food value is highest when produce is prepared just prior to serving, pre-washed cut-up carrot and celery sticks stored in the refrigerator in plastic bags will make snacking easy. For convenience, greens too can be washed, dried, and kept in a refrigerated lettuce crisper, plastic container, or closed plastic bag. You can even pre-mix the greens with chopped radish, green pepper, carrots, and celery for a standing salad base. A paper or linen towel in the bottom of the container will absorb any moisture, keeping the salad crisp and fresh for about three days. You will be surprised how often you use lettuce on a sandwich or snack on a salad when the fixings are available instantaneously. If the mix becomes too soft for salad, turn it into soup. (Do not add tomatoes, avocado, mushrooms, or other vegetables that wilt or discolor quickly until serving time. Do not add onion or scallion until serving, as their flavors will increase during storage. Do not add dressing either until serving time.)

When preparing salad dressing, make up enough to keep a jarful in the refrigerator. Designating a certain jar (or jars) for this purpose will help remind you to make more when it becomes empty.

Precooked Vegetables

When steaming a pot of vegetables, make extra. Precooked vegetables combined with a thin white sauce make excellent soup; add a thick white sauce and you have the filling for a pot pie. Marinated in oil and vinegar they become an appetizer or salad garnish. Leftover potatoes can be home-fried the next day or mashed and mixed into a potato dough.

Soup is another item easily made in extra volume; what you don't eat the first day can be extended with tomato juice or vegetable broth, enhanced with some cooked grain, pureed for "cream" soup, or simply used as the stock for cooking beans, vegetables, or grains. One pot of soup may actually provide the basis for two or three completely different meals.

Advertising Pays

Stimulate use of leftovers and foods in season by posting a "Now Featuring" list or blackboard on your refrigerator and freezer. This will provide suggestions for those who are browsing, help remind the cook of what is already there, and keep foods, unnoticed at the back of a shelf, from going to waste. In this way, too, cold air will not be wasted as hungry seekers stare into the open refrigerator for inspiration.

Organize the Cooking Schedule

Attempt only one new or complicated dish per meal, keeping the rest simple or familiar. Since timing a meal can be the most complicated part of cooking, you may even find it helpful to write out the menu and post it in the kitchen.

Think through everything that needs to be done. Any items that you store in the refrigerator, which are best served at room temperature, should be removed when you begin meal preparation. Make note of any foods that have to marinate, as you may want to prepare these first. Consider which dishes can be made and held (i.e., kept warm or cold) and which should be served immediately. Foods that can most easily sit should be prepared first, so that last-minute operations can be done without interference. Those that take the longest to cook should be given early consideration too; while they are heating, other parts of the meal can be attended to.

Energy-Saving Tricks

▪ A pot of water set to boil should always be covered. This conserves time and fuel.

▪ Unnecessarily fast boiling wastes fuel; keep heat just high enough to maintain a gentle roll. Flames should never emerge around the bottom of a pot.

▪ Always choose the smallest possible utensil or appliance to do the job. Boiling a little water in a large pot, putting a small pot on a large burner, and lighting the oven to defrost a single slice of bread are frequent violations of this rule.

▪ When using the oven, try to plan the meal so that the heat will be used for more than one dish.

▪ If the fuel wasted to preheat an empty oven disturbs you, you will be glad to know that most ovens can be turned off about 10 minutes early, as their insulation will maintain the temperature for at least five minutes. As the oven temperature slowly descends, the heat already trapped within the food will continue to cook it. However, if you suspect longer cooking will be required, leave the oven on; turning it off too soon, only to have to relight it, is less energy-efficient.

Index

There's an epidemic with 27 million victims. And no visible symptoms.

It's an epidemic of people who can't read.

Believe it or not, 27 million Americans are functionally illiterate, about one adult in five.

The solution to this problem is you... when you join the fight against illiteracy. So call the Coalition for Literacy at toll-free **1-800-228-8813** and volunteer.

Volunteer Against Illiteracy. The only degree you need is a degree of caring.